Step-by-step guide to

Google Forms

by

Barrie "Baz" Roberts

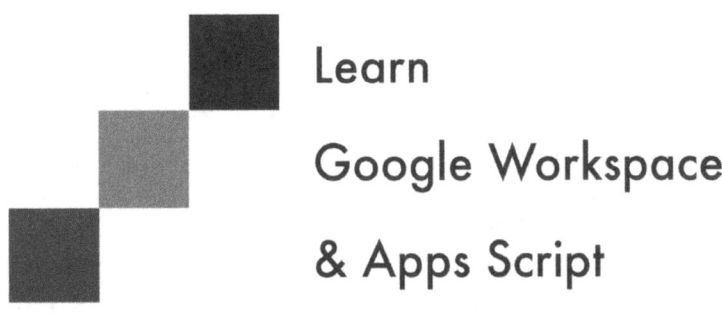

Learn

Google Workspace

& Apps Script

Contents

© *Barrie Roberts*

Introduction

Unlock the full potential of Google Forms with confidence using this guide. Follow the chapters sequentially for a structured learning experience. If you're already familiar with certain areas, jump straight into relevant chapters.

Each chapter offers clear step-by-step guides to streamline your use of Google Forms, from basics to advanced techniques. Whether you're a student or a professional, this book is your go-to resource for mastering Google Forms efficiently.

Enjoy!

Baz Roberts

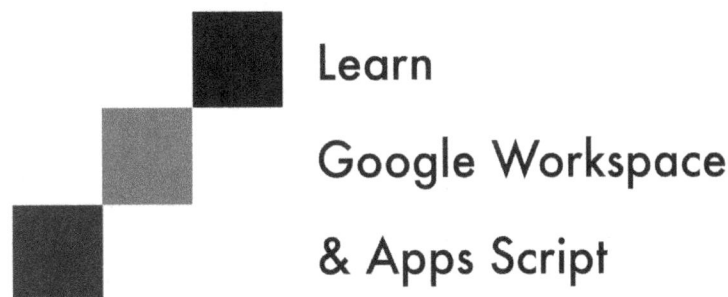

Learn

Google Workspace

& Apps Script

1: Google Forms – How do they work?

Google Forms is one of the simplest tools to use to collect data and information but as they can be connected to a spreadsheet (Google Sheet) they can be very powerful in terms of data analysis.

There are numerous uses for Google Forms but common ones are:

- Collecting feedback - questionnaire
- Signing up to an event
- Data entry - providing a more user-friendly interface
- Collecting opinions on a topic
- Collecting answers to a test

So how do they work?
A form is created with questions.

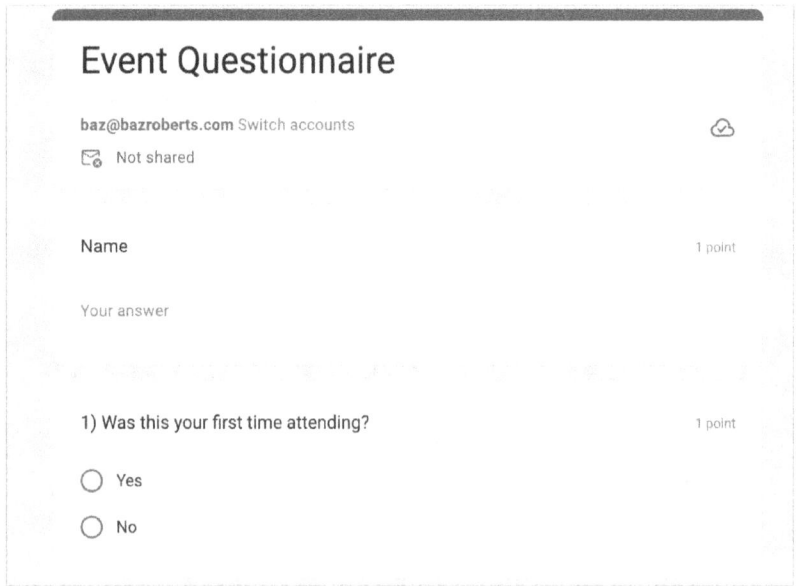

The form is filled out and is submitted.

The responses are stored in the form and they are summarised on the Responses tab.

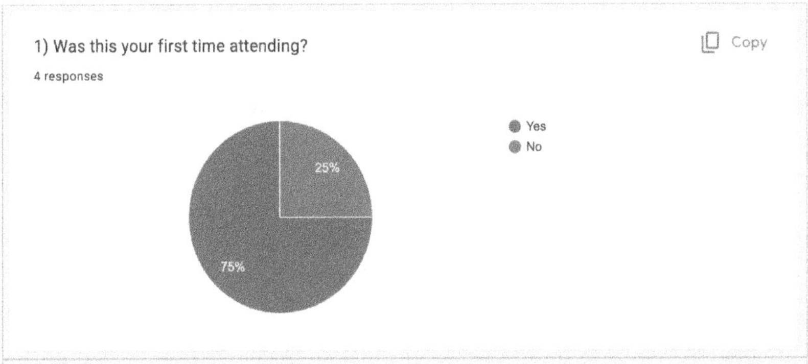

1) Was this your first time attending? Copy

4 responses

- Yes
- No

25%

75%

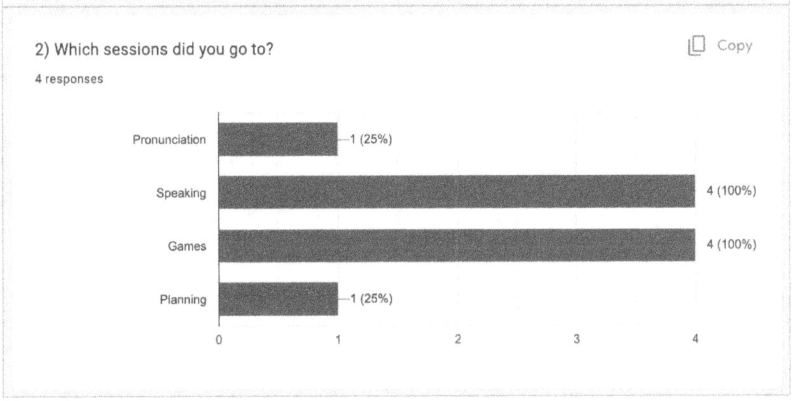

2) Which sessions did you go to? Copy

4 responses

Pronunciation — 1 (25%)

Speaking — 4 (100%)

Games — 4 (100%)

Planning — 1 (25%)

0 1 2 3 4

The form can also be linked to a spreadsheet (Google Sheet). The spreadsheet instantly populates with responses, with each row representing a respondent's answers.

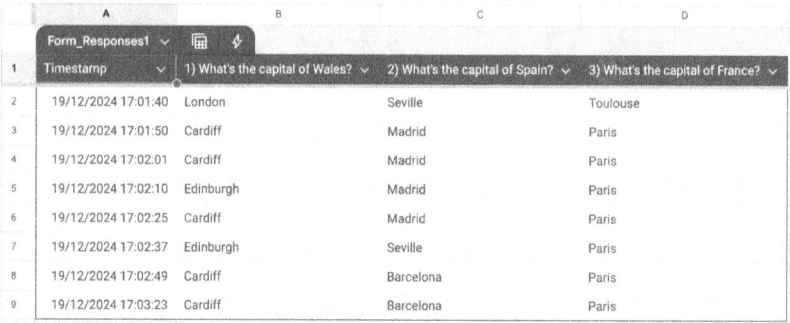

To show the responses summary from the Google Sheet, go to:

Tools > Manage Form > Show summary of responses

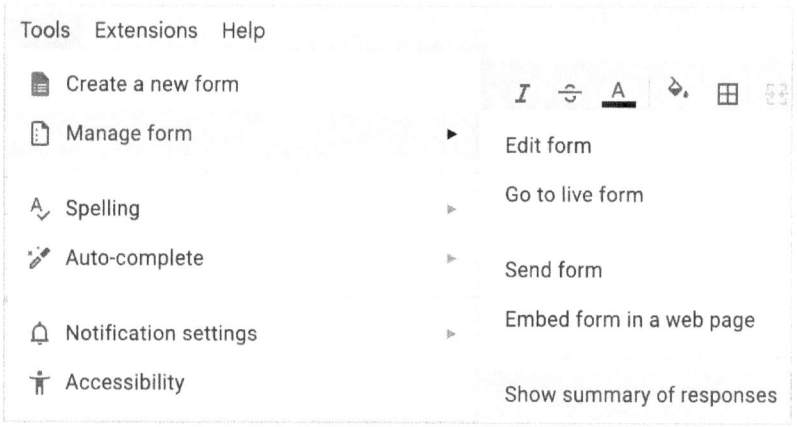

This opens the form on the responses summary page, which we saw above.

Clearing a form

If the respondent wants to clear what they have filled out on the form, they can click "Clear form".

Clear form

They just need to confirm this by clicking "Clear form" again and all their responses on all the pages will be removed.

Clear form?

This will remove your answers from all questions and cannot be undone.

Cancel   Clear form

2024 Changes to Forms

Google made some key changes to Forms at the end of 2024 and moved certain functions to new places. This book covers the new/current way but you may find forms which were created before this change and they will still use the old version of Forms, so these areas will be in different places.

2: Quick tour of Google Forms

Before we dive into the details, let's look at how Google Forms is laid out. When you create a new form you will be in the EDIT view so you can make your new form.

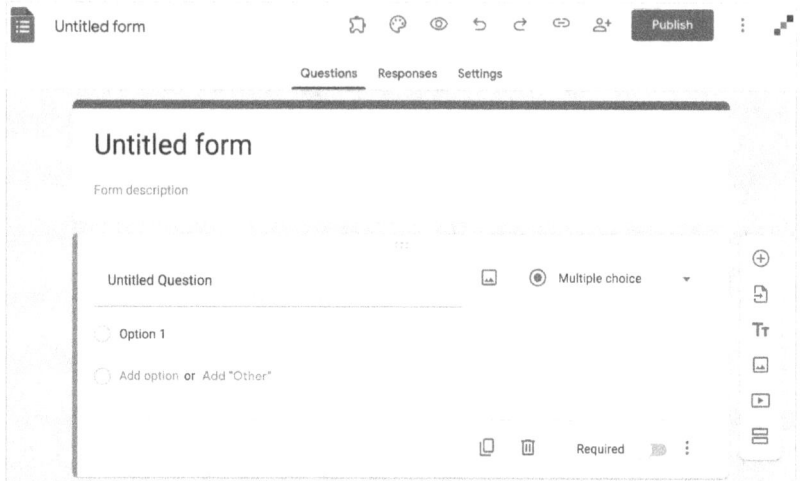

In the top-left corner you have the filename. The folder icon allows you to move the form to another folder. The star adds it to your starred files on Drive.

Clicking on the Form icon, takes you to the Forms homepage, where you can find your forms and also templates.

In the top-right you can find the following (going from left to right):

Add-ons: Lists any add-ons you may have added to Forms. These are mini-programs that extend the functionality of Forms.

Theme: To change the text style, add a header image, set the colour theme, and background colour.

Preview: This displays the form your users will see.

Undo / Redo: To undo and redo actions.

Copy responder link: To copy the form link the responders will use.

Share: To share either the link to the responder view or the editor view.

Publish: When you first create a form, it isn't published, which means no-one can fill it out.

3-dot menu: Additional options (see below).

Here, you can make a copy of the form, delete it, get a link to a pre-filled form, get the HTML to be able to embed it in a webpage, print it (and also save it as a PDF).

You can automate the form via Apps Script using the Script editor, and install add-ons, unpublish the form, and see the list of keyboard shortcuts.

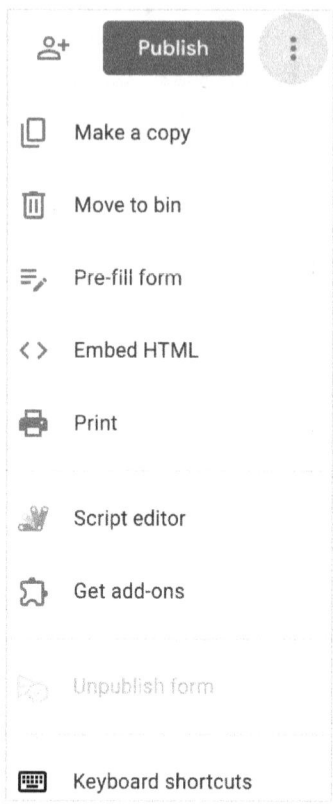

In the middle we have the main areas where you will be working, adding the questions, reviewing the responses, and changing the form settings.

In the Questions section you will find each question as a block.

On the right of the questions, you will find the questions toolbar, where you can add questions, images, videos, etc.

We'll look at the Responses once we have some responses in our form. Settings contains the global settings for the form.

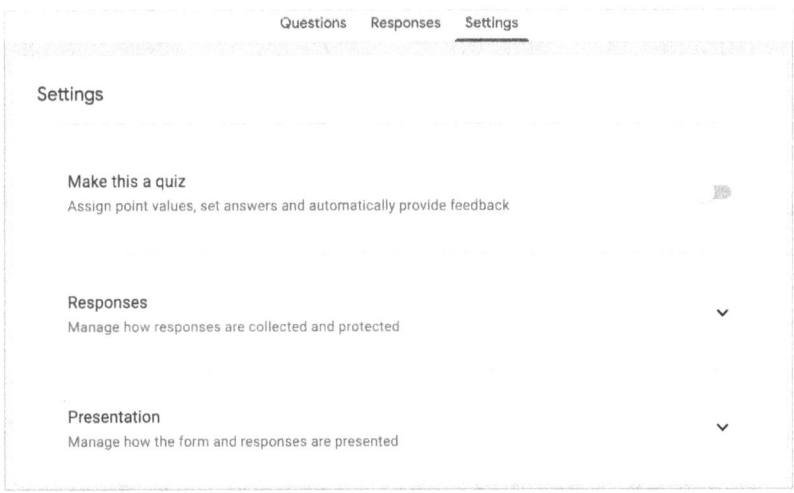

We'll look at these three tabs in more detail in later chapters.

3: Creating a form

Let's dive in and make a quick multiple-choice quiz. You'll see how easy it is to make one!

There are 4 main parts:

- Creating the form
- Adding questions
- Sharing the link
- Linking a spreadsheet to store the responses (optional)

Creating the form
In Google Drive, click on the "New" button, then "Google Forms".

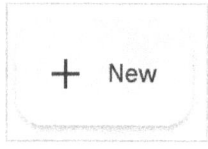

Tip: The quickest way to create a Google form in Chrome, is to type **form.new** in the address bar. Either way, you'll now be on the form edit screen and your form to edit is in the middle.

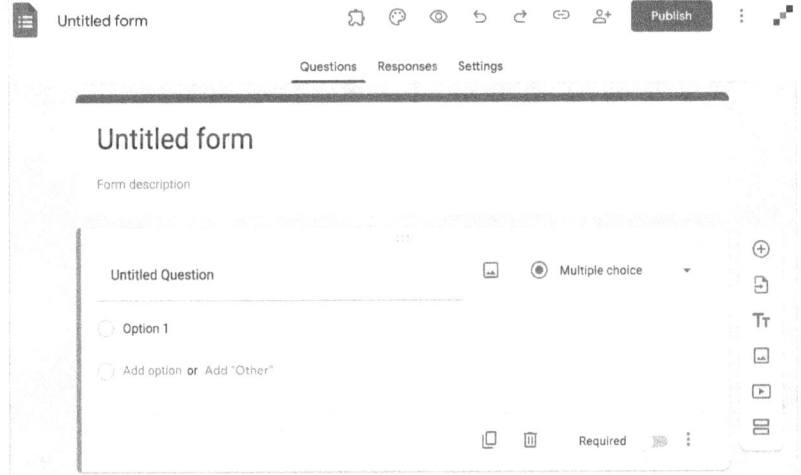

Naming the form and file

Previously, I already created a simple multiple-choice form and named it "Revision test". In the top left-hand corner, you'll notice that the file is still called "Untitled form". So, let's give it a more meaningful name.

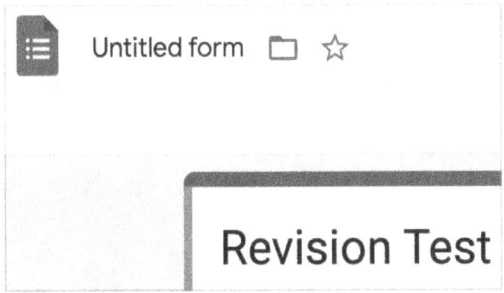

Click on the filename "Untitled form" and automatically it will suggest naming it the same as the form title. You can leave it like this, or you can press delete and type in your own filename.

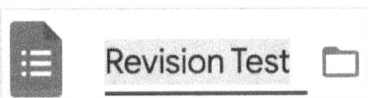

Back in the form, we can also add a form description. Click on "Form description" under the form title and type in the text you want.

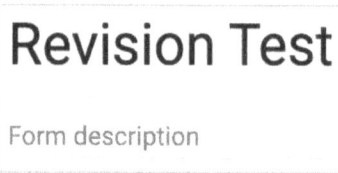

You also have some text styling options and also the option to add a numbered list and bulleted list.

Adding questions

You can give your form a title by clicking on "Untitled form" and typing in a name, e.g. "Revision Test".

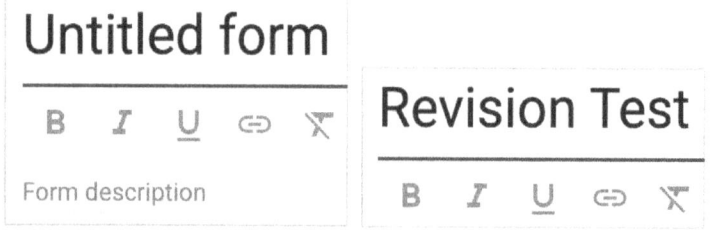

You can also add a bit of basic styling to the title text, like bolding and italics.

To add your first question, click on "Untitled Question" and type in your question.

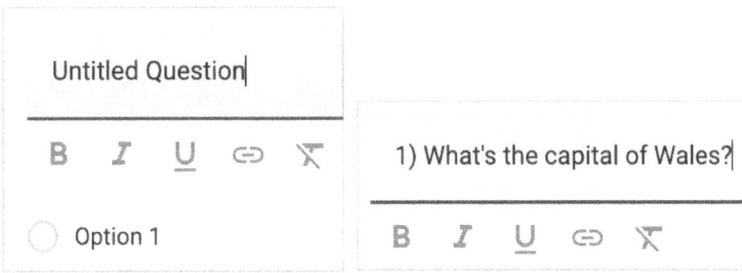

By default, the answer format is multiple-choice and that's what I want in this example. So, now we need to enter the options. Click on "Option 1" and type in a possible answer.

> ◯ Option 1
>
> ◯ Add option or Add "Other"

To add other options, either click on "Add option" or press the Enter key.

> 1) What's the capital of Wales?
> _____
>
> ◯ London
>
> ◯ Cardiff
>
> ◯ Edinburgh

Duplicating questions

To add another question, click on "Duplicate" at the bottom of the box.

I find clicking on the "Duplicate" button is usually best, as it duplicates the current question, saving you having to add the options in again and often the questions are in a similar format.

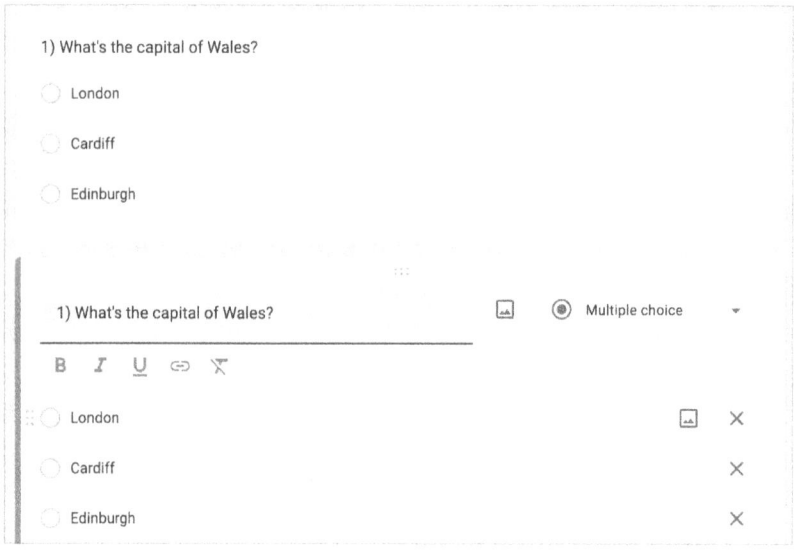

Click on the duplicated question to edit it and click on the options to edit them.

> 2) What's the capital of Spain?
>
> ○ Madrid
>
> ○ Seville
>
> ○ Barcelona|

I've duplicated the last question again and edited it to add 3 new options.

Viewing a form
Once I've finished making the form, I always check it looks ok. So, to view your form, click the eye icon at the top-right of the screen.

This will open the form on a new page in your browser, and this is what you share with those you want to fill in your form.

Revision Test

1) What's the capital of Wales?

○ London

○ Cardiff

○ Edinburgh

2) What's the capital of Spain?

○ Madrid

○ Seville

○ Barcelona

3) What's the capital of France?

○ Toulouse

○ Paris

○ Lyon

Submit   Clear form

Editor view vs Responder view

It's important to remember that there's one link to edit the form and one to view and fill out the form. You can see the difference at the end of the URL.

<u>Editor view</u>
The one which you edit the form has **/edit** on the end.

<u>Responder view</u>
And the one you fill out the form has **/viewform** at the end. If you want them to fill out your form, always share this one.

Publishing a form
To be able to be filled out, the form needs to be published. To do this, click the "Publish" button. With a normal Gmail account, by default the form can be filled in by anyone with a link.

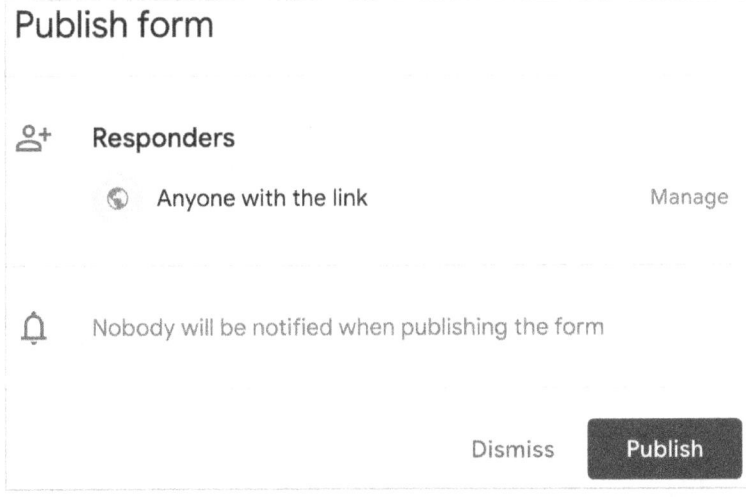

Publish form

Responders

Anyone with the link   Manage

Nobody will be notified when publishing the form

Dismiss   Publish

With paid Workspace accounts, the default is to only share the form with the organisation.

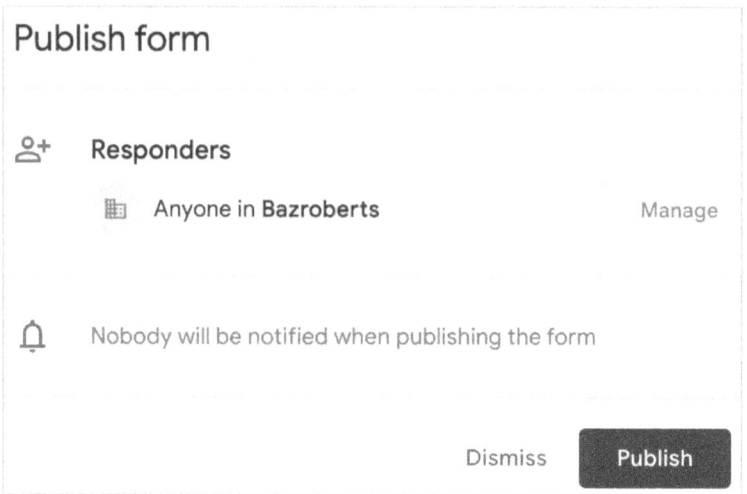

Both with Gmail and Workspace accounts, click the Publish button to publish the form. Once published, the Published icon will change to "Published" and you can control if the form accepts responses and who can respond to the form.

Creating a spreadsheet to store the responses
Forms does store the responses within the form but it's often useful to store them in a spreadsheet for easier analysis afterwards.

To connect a spreadsheet to the form, from the form edit page, click on "Responses", then click "Link to Sheets".

This will open a dialogue box asking you if you want to create a new spreadsheet or an existing one. For now, leave the default which is create a new one and click "Create".

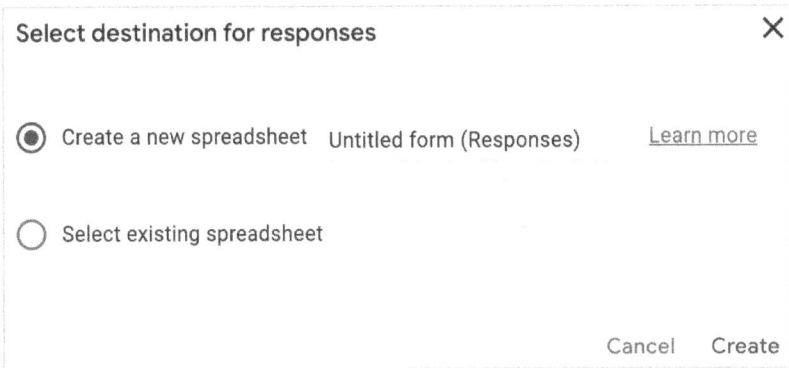

This will create a spreadsheet where your responses will be stored. The questions from your form are in row 1, along with a timestamp, which tells you when someone submitted your form.

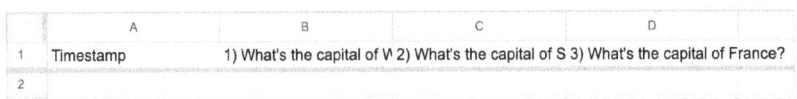

Now the form is ready to be shared!

4: Types of questions

In this chapter we're going to look at the different types of questions there are in Google Forms. In the edit view and Questions tab, click on "Multiple choice".

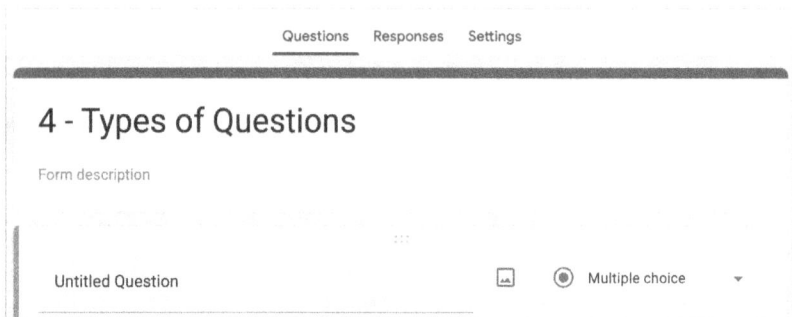

You will be presented with all the options. Click on the one that best suits.

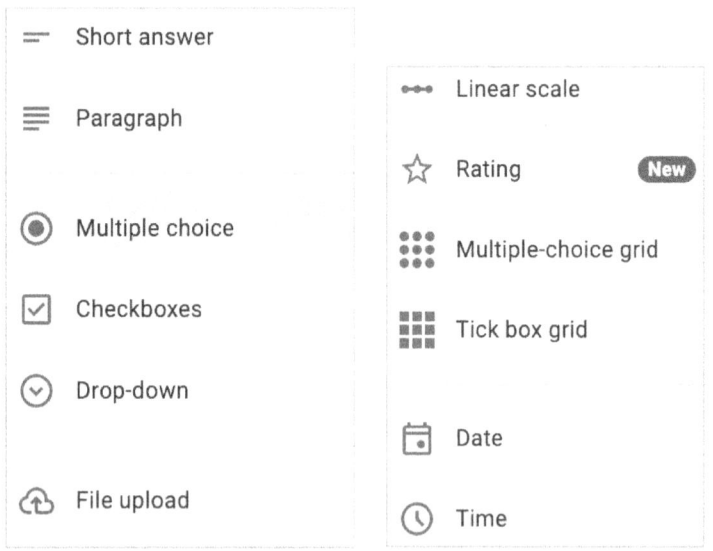

Here is a summary of what the questions look like in both the edit view and in the responder view. Plus, some tips as to when to use them.

Short answer
Use this if when you want the respondent to write a short single-line answer. They can write a longer answer, but the box is small so they can only see a few words. Type your question where it says "Untitled Question".

E.g. Typing their name; A short opinion

Untitled Question	🖼	☰ Short answer	▾
Short-answer text			

Name
Baz _____

Paragraph
This is when you want the respondent to write a longer answer. The box is bigger than a Short Answer so they can see what they've written.

E.g. Leaving comments; A longer opinion; Offering suggestions

How could we improve our service?	🖼	☰ Paragraph	▾
Long-answer text			

How could we improve our service?

I had to wait a long time before being served, so, I think installing a ticket system would be useful to cut down waiting times

Multiple choice

This is when you want to give them limited options. These are easier to analyse afterwards as these standardize the answer format, i.e. no room for interpretation or misspelling. However, in tests these are usually easier than answers which require the responder to write in an answer.

You can open up the options by offering the "Other" option, where the form filler writes in an alternative response. This can be usual in questionnaires, where you don't always know all the possible responses that the respondents will come up with.

E.g. Tests; Questionnaires (feedback & opinions)

What course do you think we should offer next?		Multiple choice	▾
◯ 80h face-to-face			✕
◯ 40h face-to-face + 40h online			✕
◯ 60h on-line			✕
◯ Other...			✕

What course do you think we should offer next?

○ 80h face-to-face

○ 40h face-to-face + 40h online

○ 60h on-line

◉ Other: Classes via Meet

Clear selection

Checkboxes
Similar to multiple-choice questions but here respondents can select more than one option.

E.g. Questionnaires; Tests where there is more than one right answer

Which sessions did you go to? ☑ Checkboxes

☐ Grammar is king ✕

☐ Vocabulary rules ✕

☐ Pron, pron and more pron ✕

☐ Listening skills ✕

Which sessions did you go to?

☑ Grammar is king

☑ Vocabulary rules

☐ Pron, pron and more pron

☐ Listening skills

Drop-down

Similar to multiple-choice questions, except that the respondent doesn't see the options until they click on the drop-down menu.

This is useful if the question has a lot of options, so you save space on your form, or where you have a lot of questions and want to save space on the page, to make the form look smaller and therefore, look quicker to fill out.

E.g. Tests, Questionnaires

Which speaker said he agreed with Mercedes?		Drop-down	▾
1. A - Ed			✕
2. B - Scott			✕
3. C - Ammar			✕
4. D - Roxanne			✕

Which speaker said he agreed with Mercedes?

Choose ▾

Choose

A - Ed

B - Scott

C - Ammar

D - Roxanne

File Upload - we'll look at this in a later chapter.

Linear scale

When you want to collect someone's opinion numerically on a scale. You can change the scale, but it must start with either a 0 or a 1, and can go up to 10.

The scale runs from the lowest on the left and the highest on the right. As this records a number, it can make analysing a bit easier than with text comments.

E.g. Opinions in questionnaires

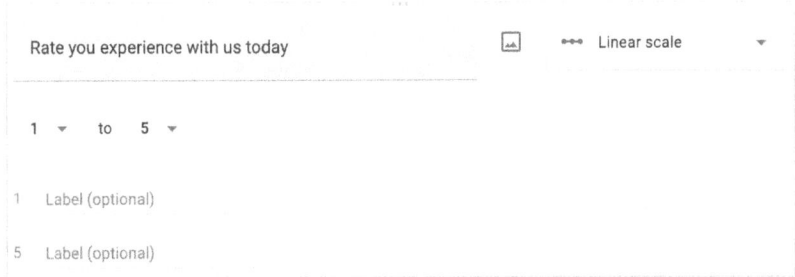

You can give the extremes a label, e.g. Poor / Excellent. Despite this, we've had times where people have misread this and assumed the left-hand side was the best, resulting in a 1 rather than a 5.

Rating

As well as the linear scale, Forms now has a specific question type for ratings. This will convert the icons into a numeric value.

The rating can be out a total from 3 to 10 and the default is 5. You also have 3 icons to choose from:

E.g. Questionnaires, surveys.

Overall rating

| 1 | 2 | 3 | 4 | 5 |

Clear selection

Multiple-choice grid

The rows are the different questions or areas, and the columns are usually the opinions, but you could set it up for other uses too. It's like having lots of multiple-choice questions joined together, grouped by a common set of options.

E.g. Questionnaires - rating various criteria on a topic

The teacher| Multiple-choice grid ▼

B *I* U̲ ⊖ ✗

Rows   **Columns**

1. Row 1   ○ Column 1

2. Add row   ○ Add column

Rows   **Columns**

1. is clear   ✕   ○ never   ✕

2. corrects my errors   ✕   ○ sometimes   ✕

3. is punctual   ✕   ○ usually   ✕

4. Add row   ○ always   ✕

You can make the form-filler add a response for each row, by clicking on the "Require one response per row" slider button.

Require a response in each row

You can also limit it to one response per column, which is good for when someone has to rank a number of items, so there's only one number one, etc.

Click on the 3-dots menu and select "Limit to one response per column".

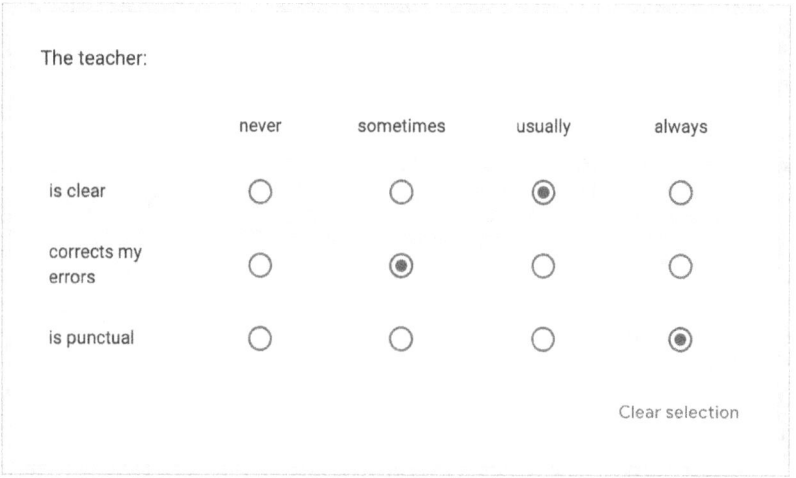

Tick box grid
Similar to the above Multiple-choice grid, you have the choice of setting up a tick box grid. The difference is that the user will be able to select multiple options per row and per column.

E.g. Finding out the best times for people; Finding out preferences from a group of people

Meeting scheduler | 🖼 | ⬛ Tick box grid | ▾

B *I* U̲ ⌖ ✗

Rows | **Columns**
1. Row 1 | ☐ Column 1
2. Add row | ☐ Add column

Rows | **Columns**
1. 10:00-12:00 | ✕ | ☐ Mon | ✕
2. 13:00-15:00 | ✕ | ☐ Tue | ✕
3. 16:00-18:00 | ✕ | ☐ Wed | ✕
4. Add row | | ☐ Thu| | ✕

As per the option above, you can also make the form-filler add a response for each row, by clicking on the "Require one response per row" slider button.

It's usually better to have the part with more options in the Rows part, rather than the Columns part, as the width of the screen is limited, whereas the form-filler can always scroll down to see further options in the Rows.

Meeting scheduler

	Mon	Tue	Wed	Thu
10:00-12:00	☑	☑	☐	☐
13:00-15:00	☐	☑	☑	☑
16:00-18:00	☐	☑	☐	☐

Date

This is when you want to record a date and possibly a time. The form-filler will be able to either type in the date or select one from the calendar by clicking on the inverted triangle.

E.g. Recording someone's date of birth, recording start and finish dates

When do you want to start classes? ⊡ 📅 Date ▾

B *I* U̲ ⌐ ✗

Day, month, year 📅

You have the option to include a time and the year.

Include time

✓ Include year

When do you want to start classes?

Date

dd/mm/yyyy ☐

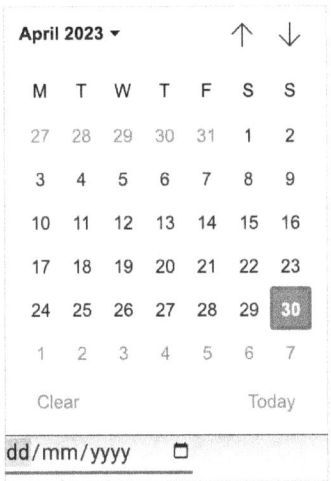

Time

Similar to the date, this is usual when you want to control the format of a time question. It's in digital format, i.e. XX:XX, but the respondent can enter the time using the 12h or 24h clock.

E.g. Referring to a specific timetable

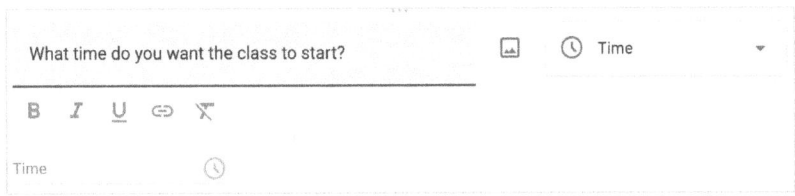

You can also ask for a duration instead of a time.

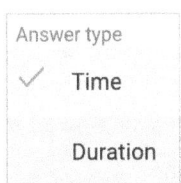

> What time do you want the class to start?
>
> Time
>
> 10 : 00

My final tip is not to include lots of different types of questions in your form. It confuses the respondent and makes the form harder work to fill out than it needs to be.

The general rule for forms is that they need to collect the information you need in the quickest time possible, as no-one likes filling in forms!

Automatic question types based on the question

Forms looks at the question you're writing and will sometimes automatically suggest possible answers for that question and change the question type accordingly.

An example is, if you type a "Do you..." question, which you would expect a yes/no answer, or possibly a maybe response. As you type the question, the suggested answers appear below. Click on the ones you want.

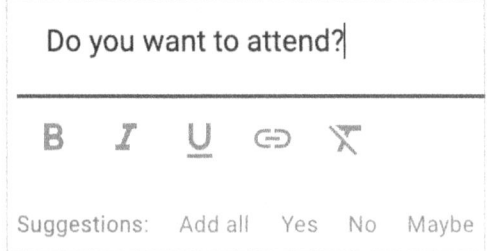

5: Questions: Other settings

In this chapter, we're going to look at:

- Making questions obligatory to complete
- Changing the order of the questions on your form
- Automatic question types based on the question

Making a question obligatory to complete
I always want them to fill in their name, so I can make the question obligatory. At the bottom of the box, click the slider button "Required", so it changes colour.

Adding a description to a question
You can add a description field to a question by clicking on the 3-dot menu in the bottom right-hand corner of the question and selecting "Description".

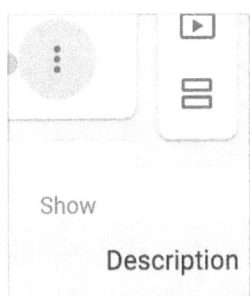

Changing the order of the questions
You can change the order of the questions by clicking on the 6 dots at the top of the question block and dragging it up or down to where you want it to be.

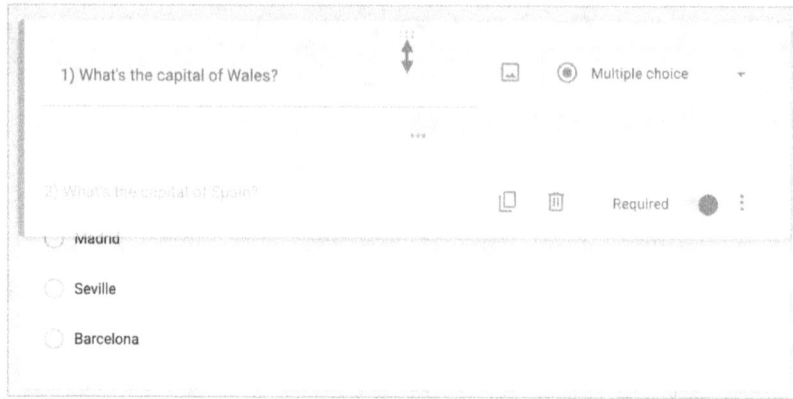

Think of each one as a separate block that can be moved around.

Deleting a question

To delete a question, just click on the trash can icon at the bottom of the question.

6: Adding titles & sections

If you've got a longer form, you'll probably want to add sections and possibly pages to your form. So, here we're going to look at:

- Adding titles
- Adding sections
- Moving sections
- Adding a long text to a question using a title

There is an important difference between titles and sections.

Titles - These add a section title to your form on the <u>current</u> page

Sections - These add a section title but put the section on a <u>new</u> page

Adding titles
On the right-hand side, there is a floating menu. Click on the double T icon to add a title to a section of your form.

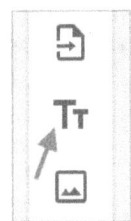

Click on "Untitled title" to give your section a name.

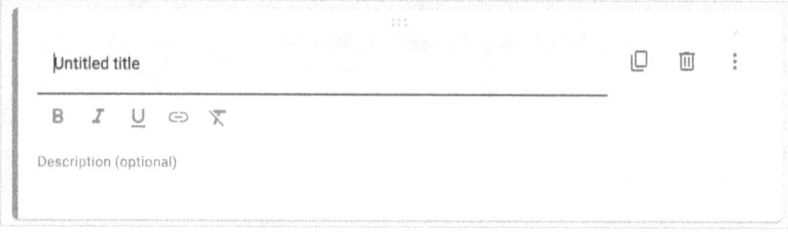

You also have the option to add a description of the section underneath.

Here's what it looks like to the user.

Section 1
Remember to read the questions carefully

Adding a new section

To add a section on a new page, click on the question you want the new section to appear AFTER. Then click Add section (two lines icon) from the floating bar.

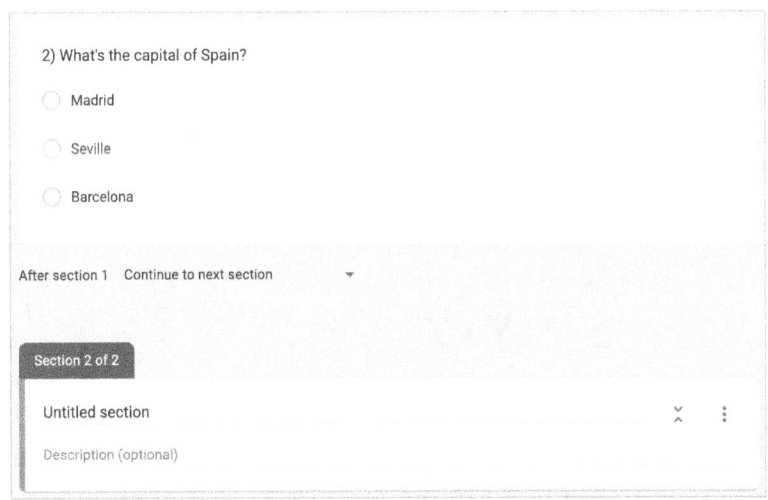

Click on "Untitled section" to change the name of the section. You can also add a description underneath.

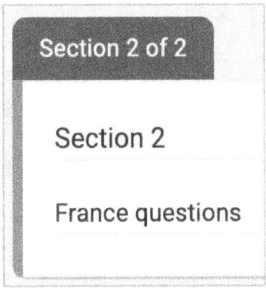

The form now has a second page and the user will need to click "Next" to move to that page.

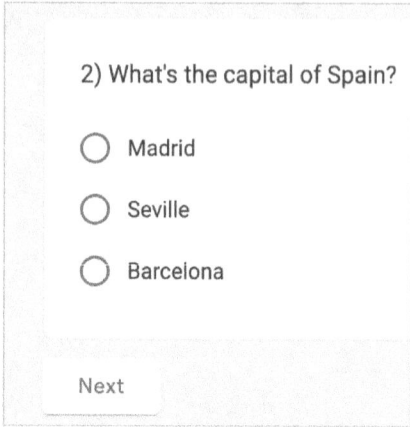

The new section looks like this:

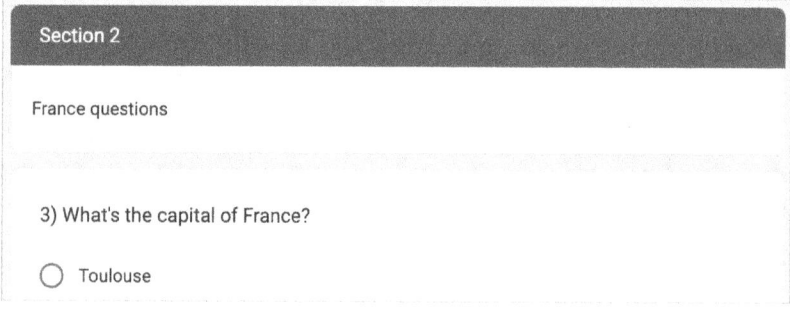

Moving sections

Moving sections is really easy. Here, I want to move section 2 before section 1.

Click on the 3-dot menu at the top of the section, then choose "Move section".

42

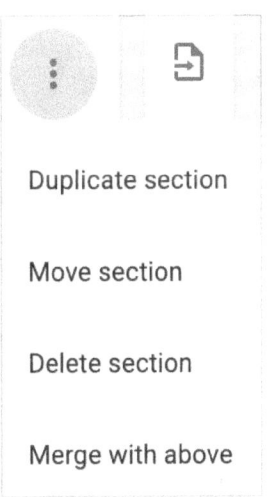

Duplicate section

Move section

Delete section

Merge with above

A pop-up box will appear. There are two ways to move the sections. Either click and hold on the 6 dots on the left of the section you want and drag it to the position you want, or click the up or down arrows on the right to move it one place up or down.

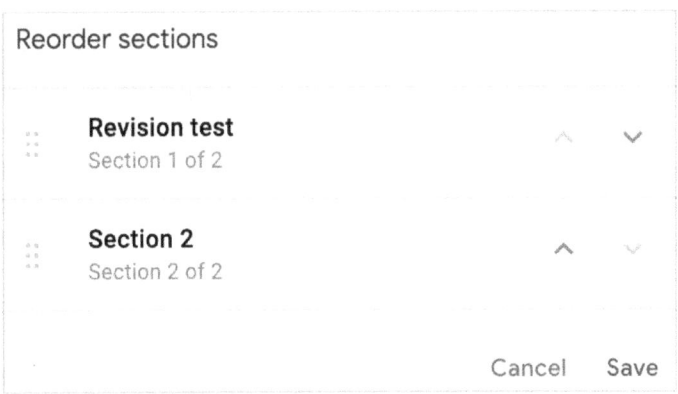

Then click "Save".

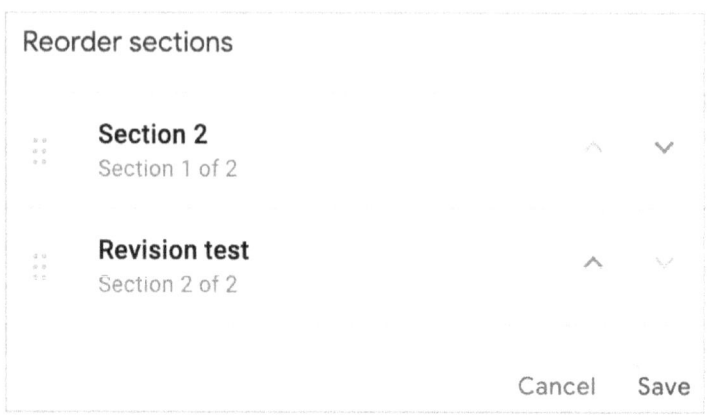

As you can see, it's moved Section 2 to Section 1.

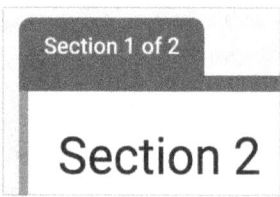

Adding a long text

If you have a text that you want your students to answer questions on, using the question option makes the text too big, but there's an alternative way. Use the "Title and description" option. Click on the double T icon from the floating menu.

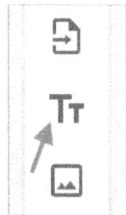

Give the question a title (optional). Then type in or paste in your text in the description box below. Note you have some formatting options to choose from. The questions are then below the text.

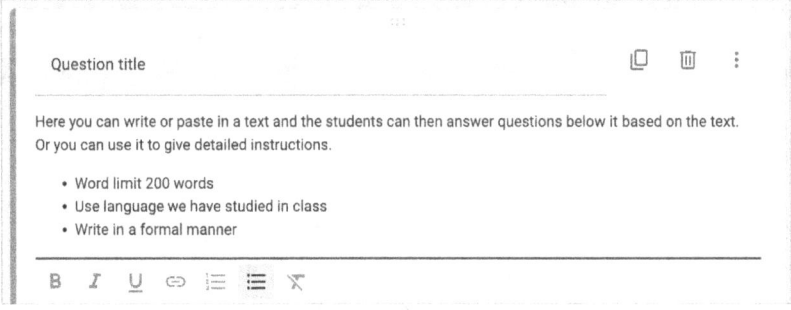

This is what it looks like on the form:

Question title
Here you can write or paste in a text and the students can then answer questions below it based on the text.
Or you can use it to give detailed instructions.

- Word limit 200 words
- Use language we have studied in class
- Write in a formal manner

7: Managing your form's responses

Once you've made your form and shared it, you'll likely want to review the responses and access a visual summary. Google Forms provides a nice graphical summary of the responses automatically right within Forms itself, so there's no need to create charts yourself.

Open your form and you'll be in the form editor. Click on the "Responses" tab. Here, it will tell you how many responses you've received and gives you the option of seeing a summary of them, seeing a summary per question, or seeing the individual responses.

To start with we'll use a post-event questionnaire as an example.

Viewing a summary of the responses
Click on the "Summary" tab. Here, you'll see all the typed in responses and for questions where there were limited options, you'll see a graph.

In this question, I can quickly see how many people had attended the event for the first time.

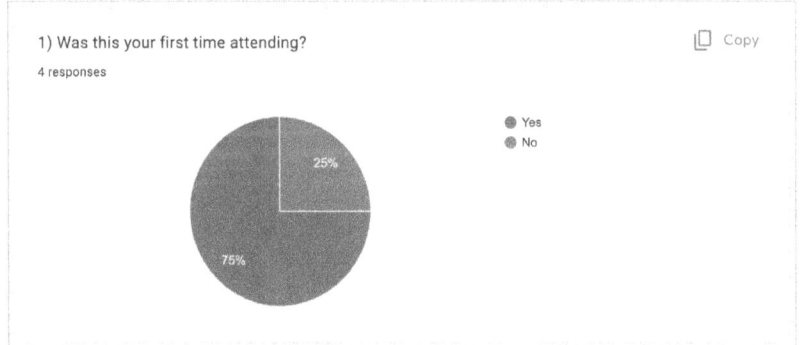

This one was a Checkbox question and I can quickly see the most popular sessions at this event.

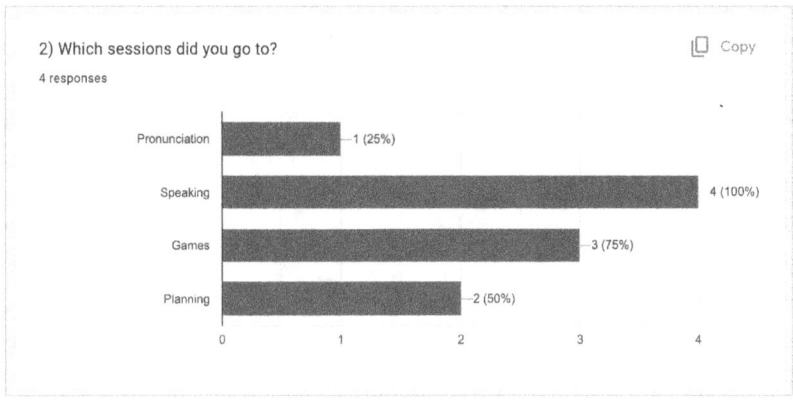

This question was a linear-scale question. Here, I can see that our customers are happy.

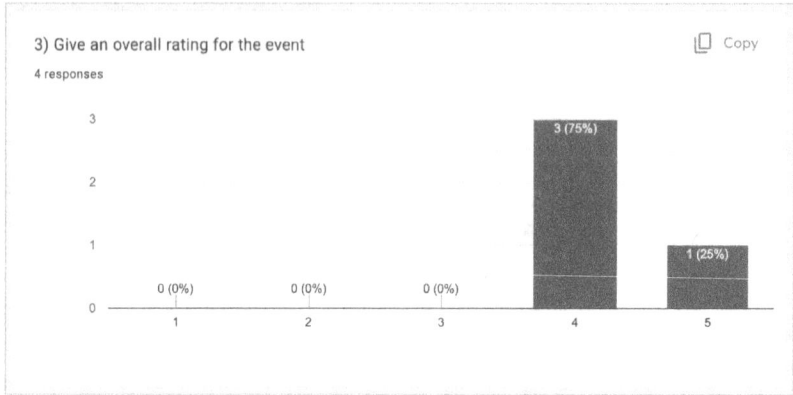

This question was a multiple-choice grid and within one graph can show a lot of information. In this case, we asked them to rate the speakers on a set of criteria.

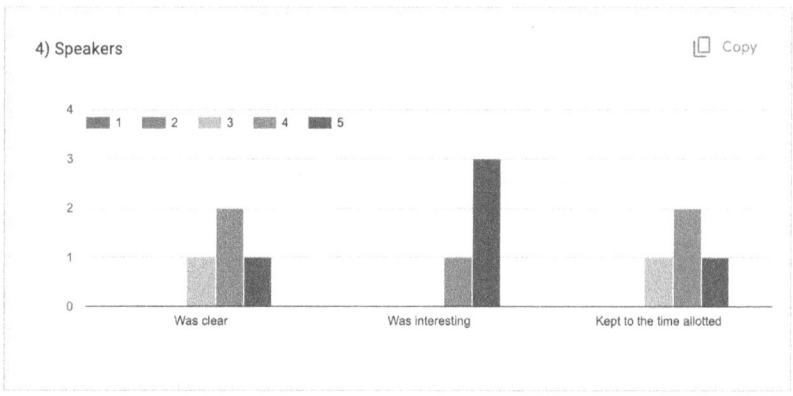

With date and time questions, Forms will put the date or time entered along with the number of people who entered it, so you can see the most popular one.

5) When do you want the next event?

4 responses

Jun 2023 | 4 2   11 2

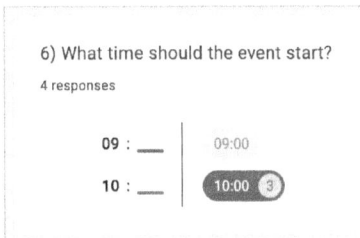

6) What time should the event start?

4 responses

09 : ___   09:00

10 : ___   10:00 ③

Viewing responses by question

You can also see a summary of the responses grouped by question. Click on "Question" to do this.

Let's look at the responses of the revision test.

You have the choice of clicking through the questions one by one using the arrows on the right, or you can go to a particular question using the drop-down menu on the left.

1) What's the capital of Wales?

2) What's the capital of Spain?

3) What's the capital of France?

In this revision test, I can see the answers my students have entered and see that lots got the answer wrong (London). So, I quickly know that we need to cover this in class.

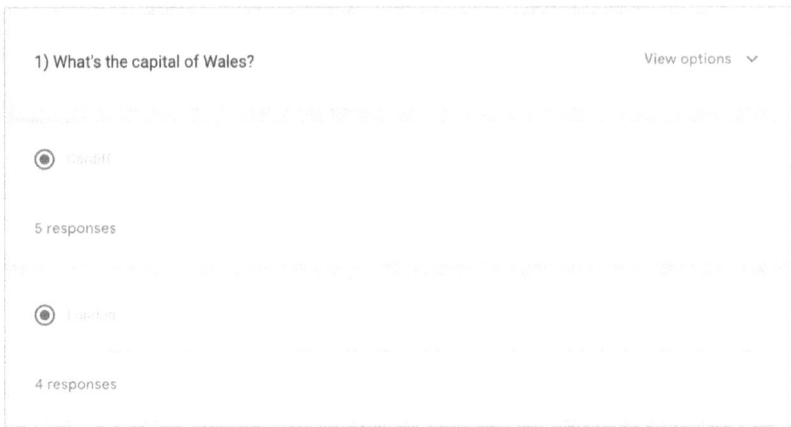

For multi-choice and checkbox questions, you also have the option to see the options that were available for that question by clicking on "View options".

Viewing individual responses

If you want to see what a specific person filled out on your form, click on "Individual". You can flick through the responses by clicking on the arrows next to where it says. e.g. "1 of 9".

This shows you exactly what the form-filler completed. It also gives you the option of deleting a response, by clicking on the bin icon on the right. Also, you can print them out.

Responses cannot be edited

Revision Test

End of unit 1 test

* Indicates required question

1) What's the capital of Wales? *

○ London

◉ Cardiff

○ Edinburgh

2) What's the capital of Spain?

◉ Madrid

○ Seville

○ Barcelona

3) What's the capital of France?

○ Toulouse

◉ Paris

○ Lyon

Submitted 01/05/2023, 11:59

Accepting responses

You can control if a form accepts responses or not by clicking on the "Published" button then toggling "Accepting responses" on or off. When turned off, if the responder opens the form, they will get a message saying this form is no longer accepting responses.

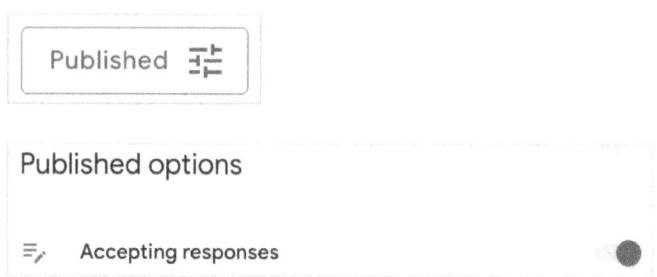

Linking responses to a Google Sheet

You can link the form responses to a Google Sheet allowing you to further analyse them. Go to the Responses tab and click "Link to Sheets".

You then have the choice of creating a new spreadsheet (and naming it) or adding a new page to an existing spreadsheet.

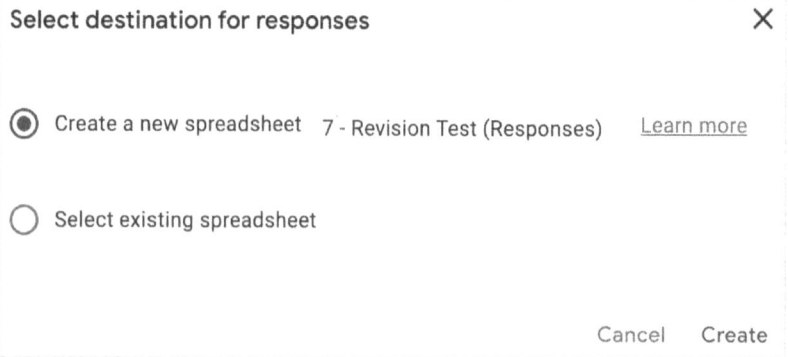

If you want a new one, just click "Create" and this will create a new spreadsheet.

If you want it to add to an existing one, click "Select existing spreadsheet". This option opens up a dialogue box where you can choose the spreadsheet you want by clicking on it, then click "Select".

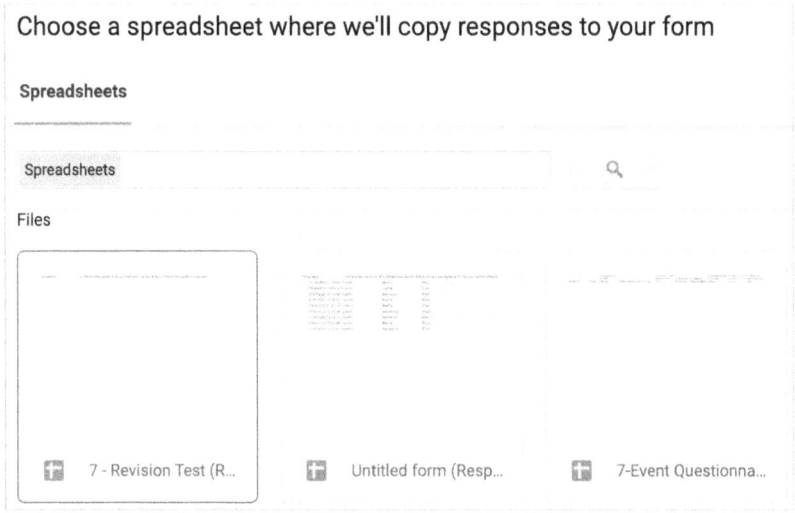

If you've already set up a spreadsheet, "Link to Sheets" will now show "View in Sheets".

Clicking on this will open the spreadsheet where the responses appear and live. Note, since 2024 it automatically creates a table in Google Sheets making it easier to analyse the data.

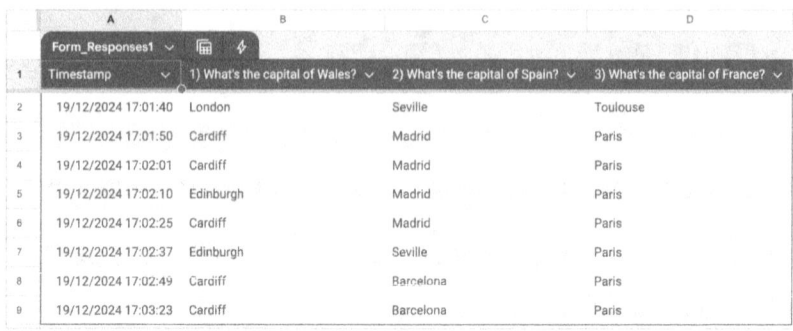

Timestamp	1) What's the capital of Wales?	2) What's the capital of Spain?	3) What's the capital of France?
19/12/2024 17:01:40	London	Seville	Toulouse
19/12/2024 17:01:50	Cardiff	Madrid	Paris
19/12/2024 17:02:01	Cardiff	Madrid	Paris
19/12/2024 17:02:10	Edinburgh	Madrid	Paris
19/12/2024 17:02:25	Cardiff	Madrid	Paris
19/12/2024 17:02:37	Edinburgh	Seville	Paris
19/12/2024 17:02:49	Cardiff	Barcelona	Paris
19/12/2024 17:03:23	Cardiff	Barcelona	Paris

Further form response options

There are also some other useful options by clicking on the 3 dots next to "View in Sheets".

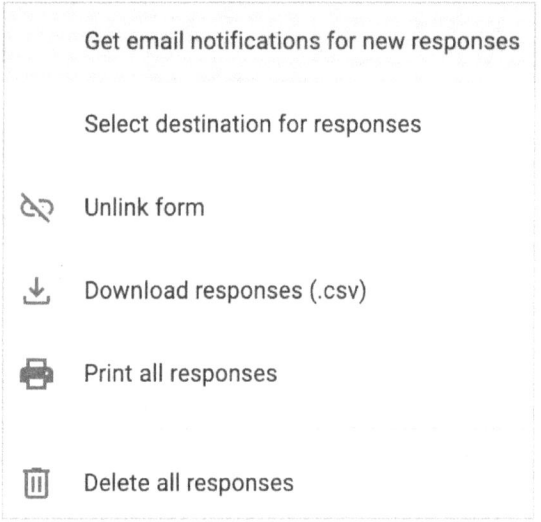

Get email notifications for new responses

Select destination for responses

Unlink form

Download responses (.csv)

Print all responses

Delete all responses

Get email notifications for new responses - By selecting this, Forms will send you an email every time someone fills out and submits your form.

Select destination for responses – Here, you can change the Google Sheet the responses will be stored on.

Unlink form - Choose this if you want to disconnect a form from a Google Sheet, so future responses won't be stored on the Sheet.

Download responses (.csv) - This downloads the responses in .csv format which can be useful for uploading the data to another application.

Print all responses – You can print all the responses or save them all as a PDF.

Delete all responses - Sometimes you want to use your form with a different set of people, e.g. a new class, but you don't want to mix the old and new responses. So, here you can delete all the responses from the form. Note, this deletes them from the form but those already collected in the spreadsheet remain.

8: Settings menu

Once you've got to grips with the basics, it's time to look at other ways you can make you form better. Let's look at further settings Google Forms provides, which are very easy to use but will allow you to use Forms in different ways.

Let's start with what's in the **Settings** tab, which you can find at the top of the edit page.

Questions   Responses   **13**   Settings

There are two main sections, Settings and Defaults.

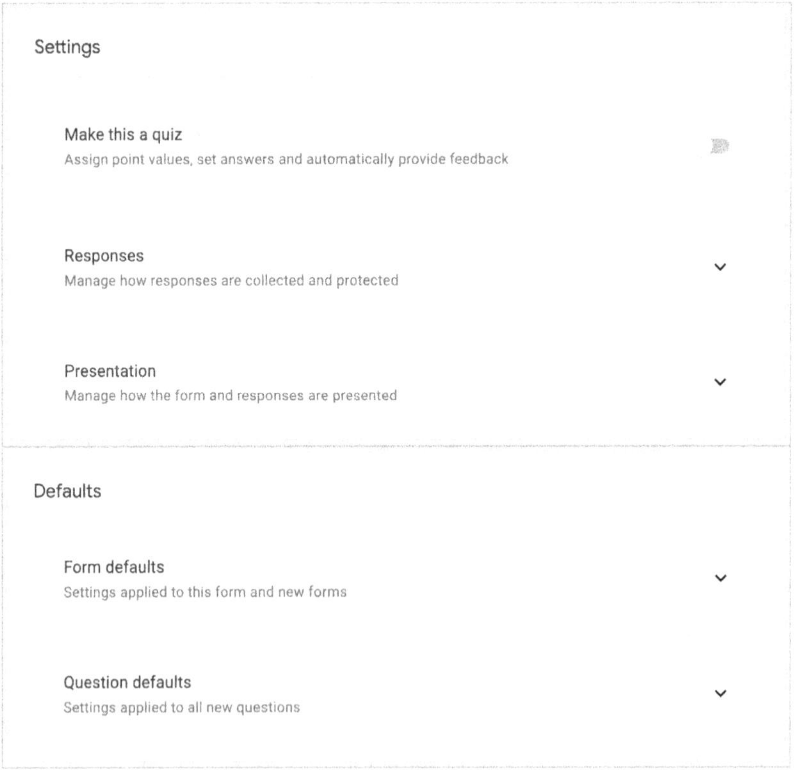

Settings

Make this a quiz
Assign point values, set answers and automatically provide feedback

Responses
Manage how responses are collected and protected

Presentation
Manage how the form and responses are presented

Defaults

Form defaults
Settings applied to this form and new forms

Question defaults
Settings applied to all new questions

Settings

In the Settings section, you can set the form up as a quiz, which we will look at in detail in a later chapter.

Responses

Next, there are options for the form responses. Click on the little arrow on the right-hand side to open the menu.

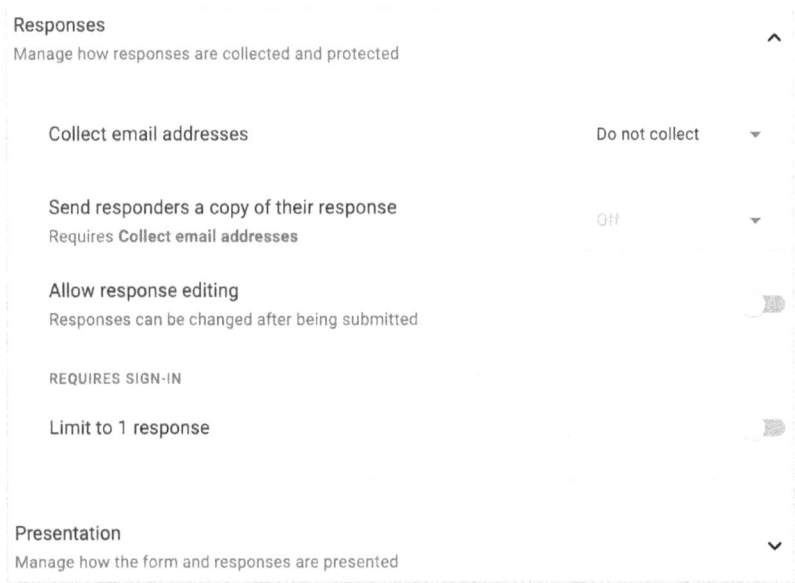

Collect email addresses - This creates a question at the top of the form to collect the user's email address. It also automatically checks that it is a valid email address.
There are 3 options:

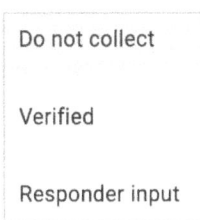

Do not collect – Doesn't ask for their email address

Verified – This will need to sign into their Google account.

Responder input – The respondent will need to enter their email address.

Collect email addresses
Required to **send response copies**
Respondents will manually enter their email response   Responder input ▾

Send responders a copy of their response - This will allow you to also send the responders a copy of their response, which can be turned on, but to do this you also need to turn Collect email addresses on.

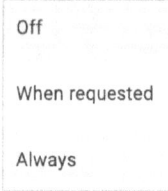

When requested – The respondent will have to enter their email address and has the option of receiving a copy of their responses or not.

Email *

Your email address

Send me a copy of my responses.

Always – The respondent will need to tick to confirm their email address, which is the one they have logged in.

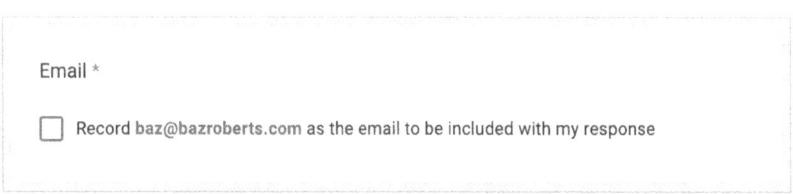

Email *

☐ Record baz@bazroberts.com as the email to be included with my response

The message at the bottom of the form tells them that they will get a copy of their responses.

A copy of your responses will be emailed to baz@bazroberts.com.

Allow responses editing – Turning this on will allow responders to edit their responses after they submit them.

Revision Test

www.bazroberts.com

Edit your response ⬅—

Limit to 1 response - This ensures a person can only send one response, but to do this they have to have signed-in to Google.

Limit to 1 response
Respondents will be required to sign in to Google.

Presentation

The final section in Settings is Presentation and this controls some of the things the responder will see on the form.

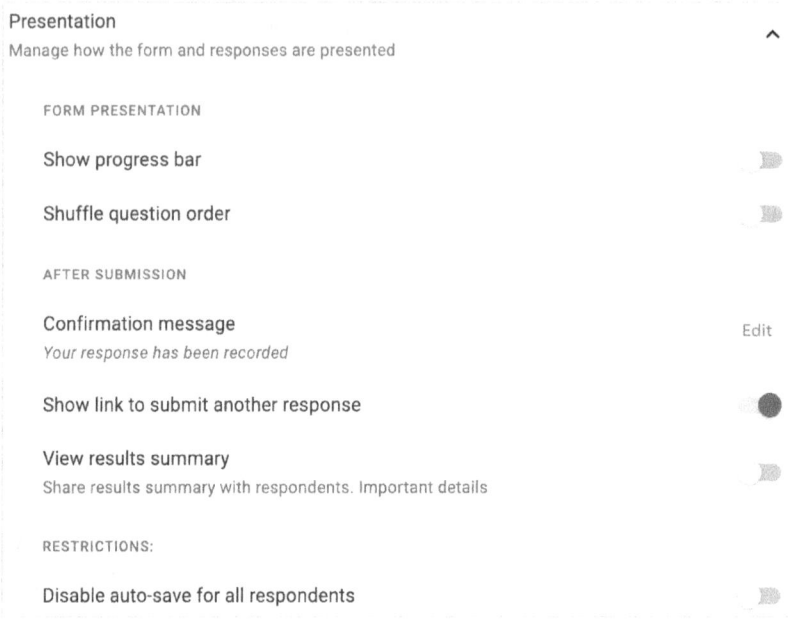

Form presentation

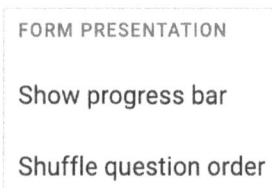

Show progress bar – You can add a progress bar to your form, which is useful if you have lots of pages, and you want to encourage those filling it out that the end is in sight!

Progress bar on the form:

Shuffle question order – You can also shuffle the question order.

After Submission

AFTER SUBMISSION

Confirmation message
Your response has been recorded

Show link to submit another response

View results summary
Share results summary with respondents. Important details

Confirmation message - By default, once the respondent has clicked Submit, they will receive a message saying "Your response has been recorded". You can change this to provide a message suitable for your situation. To change it, click Edit and type it in the message.

Tip: You can add links here, e.g. a link to a page on Google Drive with the answers to a test.

When the form is submitted, the user sees this on the confirmation page:

Revision Test

www.bazroberts.com

Show link to submit another response - You can give them the opportunity to submit another response. This appears when they submit the form.

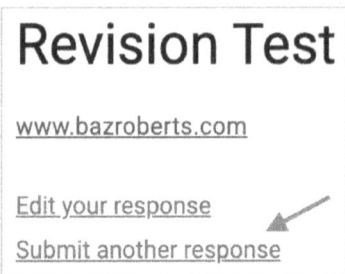

View results summary – You can share a summary of the form results with the respondents.

Restrictions
The final part is to disable the auto-save function on Forms.

By default, if the respondent is signed-in, their responses are saved as they fill in the form. This can be useful for longer forms where they don't have to fill it in all-in-one go.

RESTRICTIONS:

Disable auto-save for all respondents

Defaults

In the second section in Settings, you can set up some global default option to your form, which can save you time when creating the form. There are two parts: Form defaults and Question defaults.

Form defaults

Collect email addresses by default – Turning this on will add the email collection on for this form and for all new forms. You can always turn it off later.

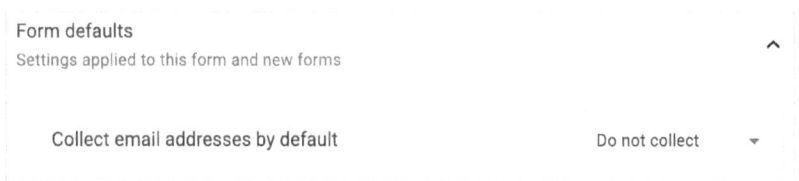

We have the same 3 options as we saw in responses.

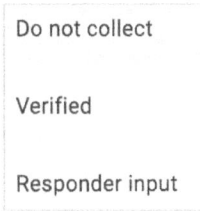

Question defaults

Make questions required by default – This makes all new questions added required by default.

Question defaults
Settings applied to all new questions

Make questions required by default

9: Adding images and videos

In Google Forms, apart from text, we can add images and videos to enrich the form, and as always this is simple to do.

Adding an image to a form

To add images to your form, click on the Image icon on the floating bar on the right-hand side.

This opens the "Insert image" dialogue box. Choose one of the options at the top depending on where your image is.

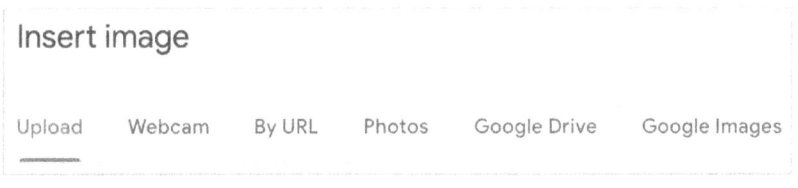

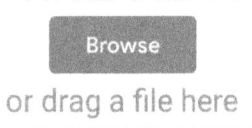

In this example, I'm going to add an image that is on My Drive. Type in the name of the file and press Enter.

Double-click on the image you want or click on it and click on "Insert" at the bottom of the box.

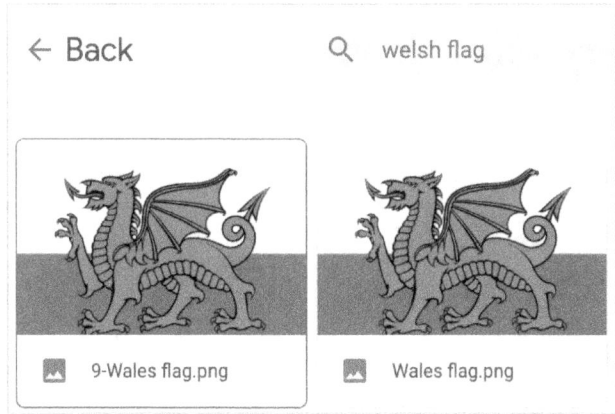

Changing the size and position of the image

This adds the image on your form. At first, it may be the wrong size. Just click on it and drag a corner of it to change the size.

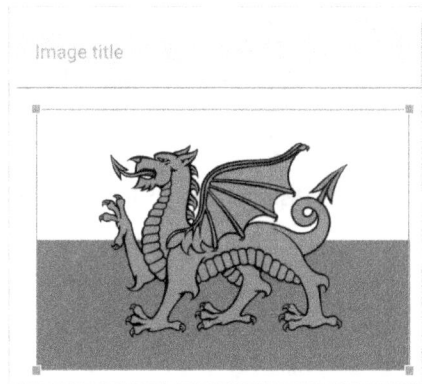

You also have the option of aligning it to the left, centre or right, and adding a title to the image. Click away from the image and you will see a 3-dot menu appear.

Click on that and the alignment options will appear. You can also change or delete the image from here.

Duplicating and deleting images

You can duplicate or delete the image by clicking on the duplicate icon or the trash can icon.

Adding a video to a form
On the floating menu, click the play icon, "Add video".

Either you can type in a search term or paste in a YouTube URL. Here, I've typed in a search. Select the video you want and click "Select".

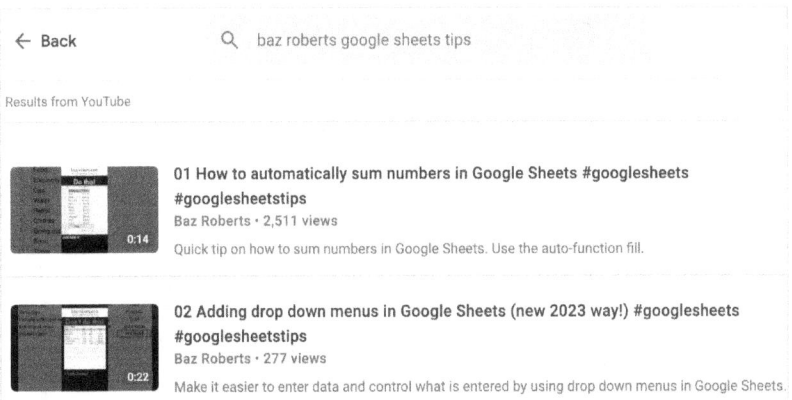

Back on the form edit page, similar to the image, you can align it and give it a title.

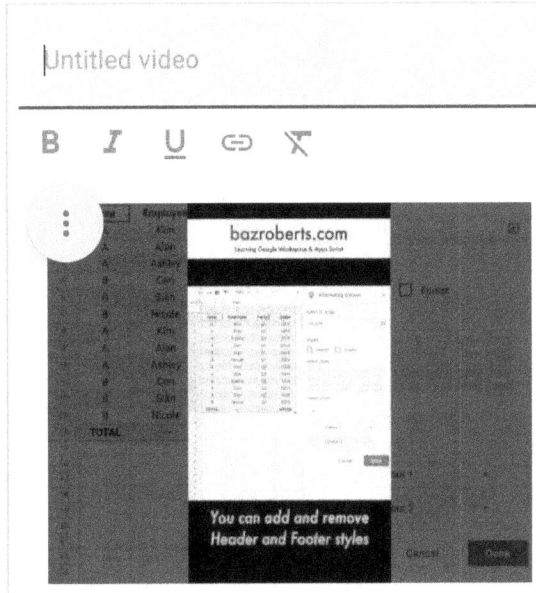

On the right, clicking on the 3 dots, gives you the option to add a caption under the video. This can be a better option than adding a big title.

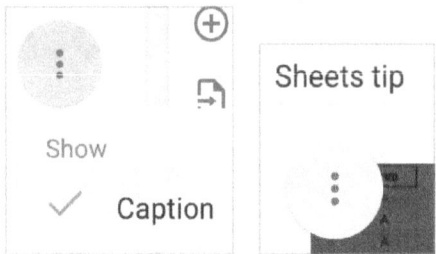

The responder will see the video embedded in the form and they will just need to click the play button to watch it.

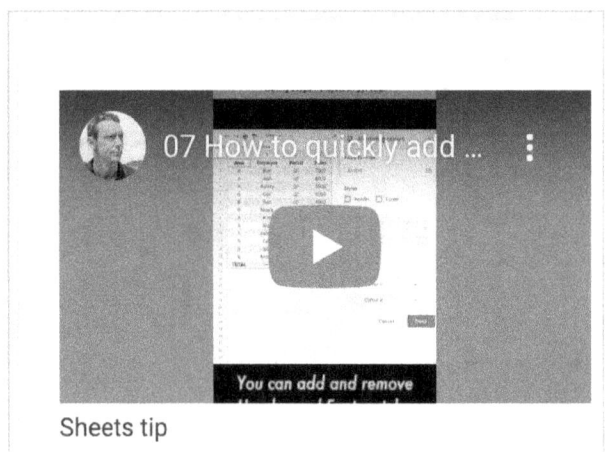

Sheets tip

10: Changing the theme

We can make Google Forms a little prettier by changing the font, header and colours, so that it can look a little more fun or professional.

Changing the form theme
By default, your form will be purple and use the Roboto font. To style it the way you want, click on the palette icon.

A sidebar will appear, where you can control the font, the header image, and colours.

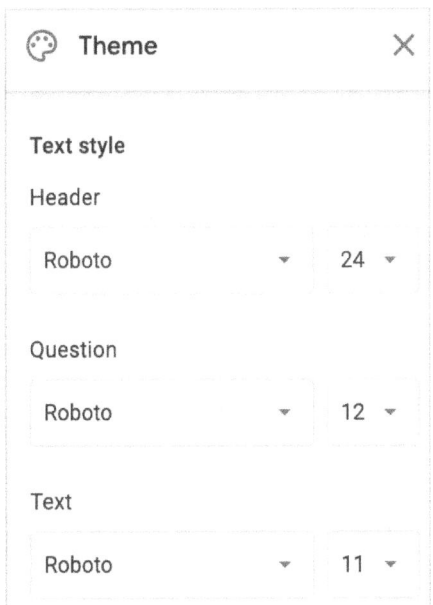

Editing the font and font size

You can change the font of the header, the question titles, and the other text on the form. Plus, you can control the font sizes. Changing the font and size can create a very different look.

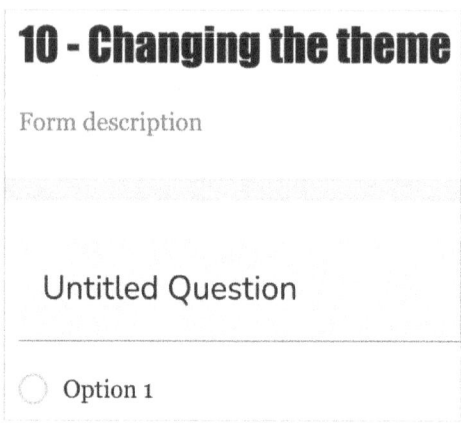

Adding a header template

By default, there is no image in the header, but we can add one. Under header, click "Choose an image".

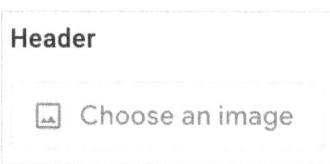

Here, you'll see various images you can use and also the option to upload your own image.

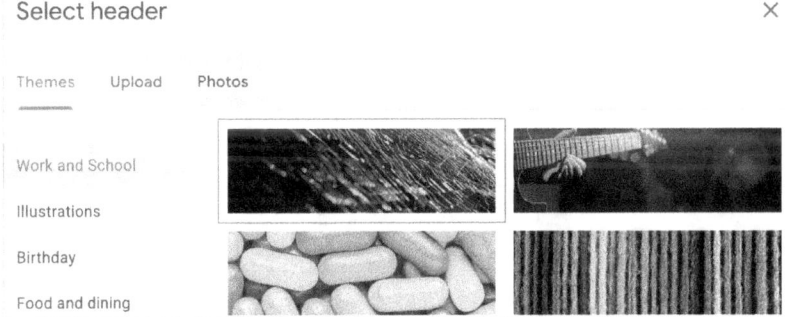

Select header   ✕

Themes   Upload   **Photos**

Work and School

Illustrations

Birthday

Food and dining

Let's start by adding a pre-set theme. Choose one of the images from one of the categories. Click the image and click the "Insert" button.

This will add the header.

It also updates the overall theme, so that the theme colours and background colours match the image.

Changing the theme colours

On the sidebar, we can change the colours by clicking on one of the circles.

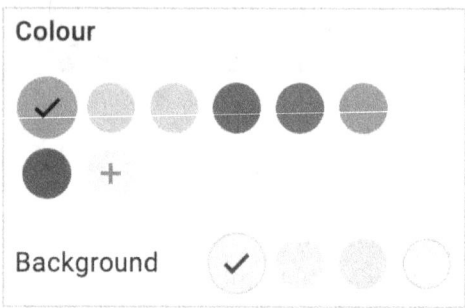

The background options are shades of the main colour selected.

We can also see it lets us know an image has been uploaded.

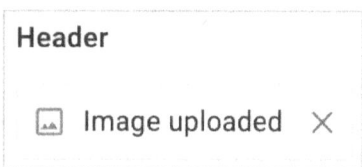

Adding your own header image

We can also upload our own photos. From the "Select header" menu, click on "Upload".

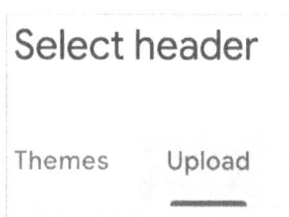

Click "Browse" or as it states, drag a file onto the dialogue box.

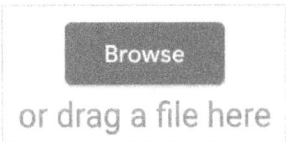

Select your photo and click "Open".

Choose your photo and once uploaded, you can crop it so it fits on the screen correctly. Just move the rectangle to the part of the photo you want to show, and then click "Done".

Long, narrow photos are best; a 4:1 aspect ratio is recommended (e.g. 800 x 200 pixels). As we can see it's changed the header image. If the image isn't the 4:1 ratio, it may crop it.

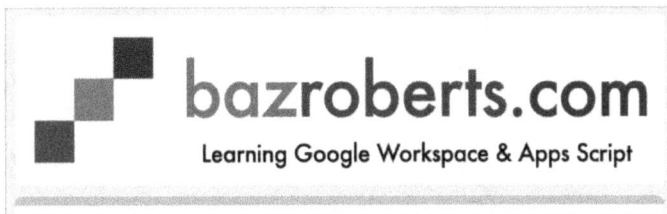

When you upload your own image, the theme and background colours change to try to match them.

Setting a new theme colour

You're not limited to the palette of colours, if you click on the + circle, this will allow you to choose a full range of colours.

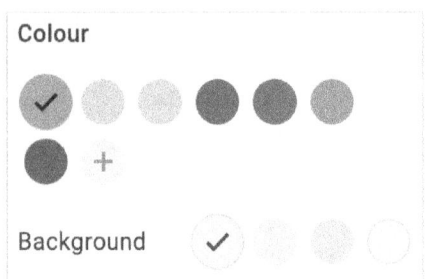

You also have the option of entering the colour as a hexadecimal code, if you want to be precise and get an exact colour. This is particularly useful if you have corporate colours and you want the forms to match them. Pick a colour then click "Add".

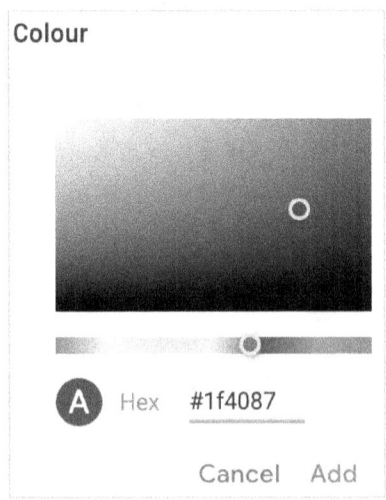

11: Sharing a form

Unless your form is for personal use, you'll want to share it with people. There are three main ways to do it:

- Share the form – Edit view &/or responder view
- Share a full or shortened link – Responder view
- Embed it in a website

Open your form and click the Sharing icon in the top-right of the screen, to open the Sharing dialogue box.

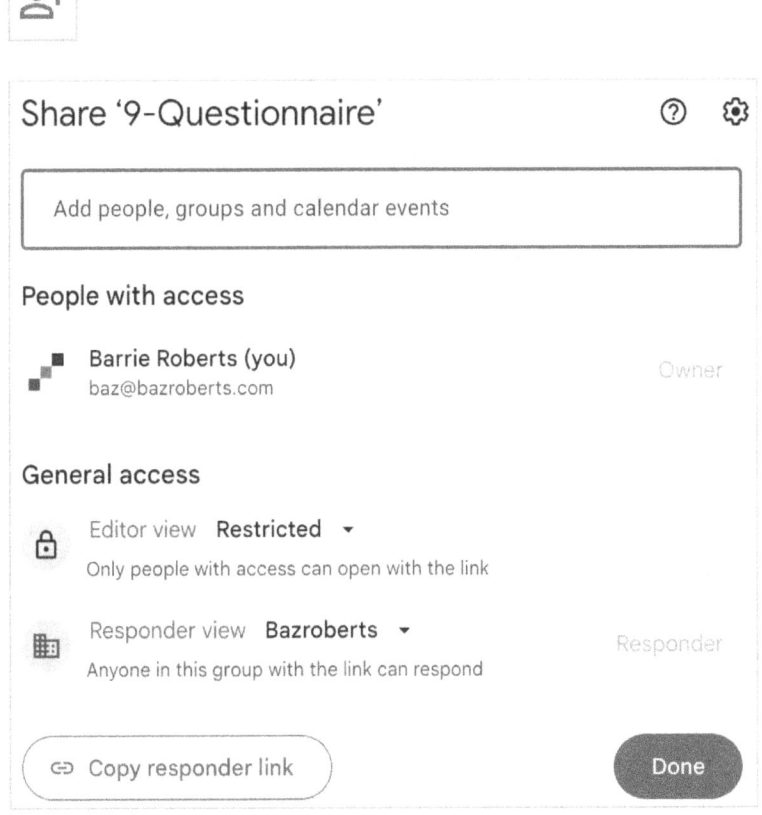

This is split into two main parts: "People with access" and "General access". The first is to share the form with specific people or groups, and the second is to share either the edit view or responder view in a general way.

Sharing the form with specific people
To share it with specific people, just type in the "Add people..." box either their names or email addresses.

You have the choice to share the edit view or responder view. Plus, you can also set an expiry date and time. Furthermore, you can notify the people that you are sharing this and add an optional message. Then click "Send".

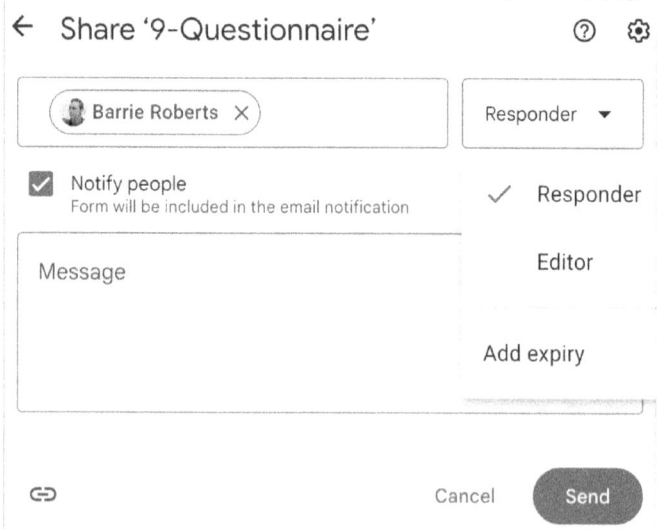

Setting an expiry date to access

To limit access for a period of time, click "Add expiry" and then set a date and time.

Setting general access to the form

This section is divided into the two different form views, so you can control the access to the editor view and the responder view.

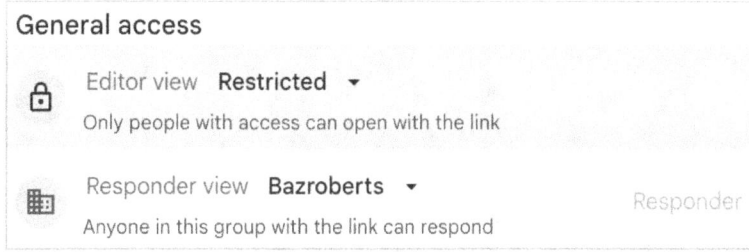

The first option is the editor view and by default it's restricted to the people you have shared the form responder view with in the section above. You can change this to share the form with your organisation (Workspace accounts only), or with anyone with the link. This then allows those people to be able to edit the form, so share it with care.

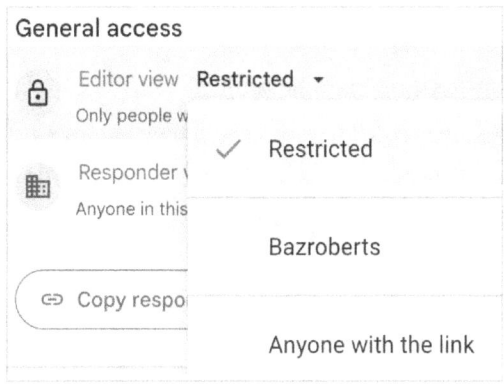

The second section is the responder view, which has the same options as above, and controls who can fill the form out. Plus, you can remove access from here by choosing "Remove link".

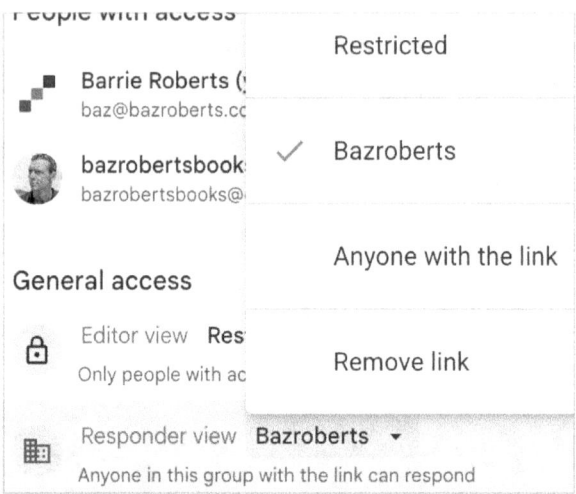

Copying the responder link
The easiest way to get the responder link is to click on the link icon at the top of the screen.

Here you can either use the full URL or get it shortened by clicking "Shorten URL". It's not the shortest of links! Click "copy" or Ctrl+C to copy the link to the clipboard, then paste it wherever you need it.

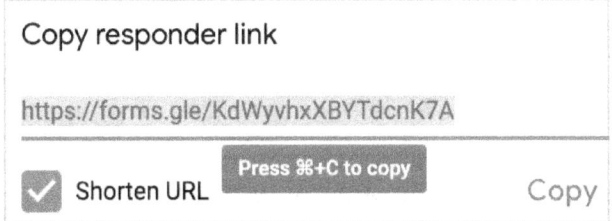

Copy responder link

https://forms.gle/KdWyvhxXBYTdcnK7A

☑ Shorten URL   Press ⌘+C to copy   Copy

Embedding your form

You can embed the form into a website like Google Sites. To get the HTML code to do this, click on the 3-dot menu at the top of the page and click "Embed HTML". You have the option to set the width and height beforehand. Just click "Copy" to copy the code to the clipboard.

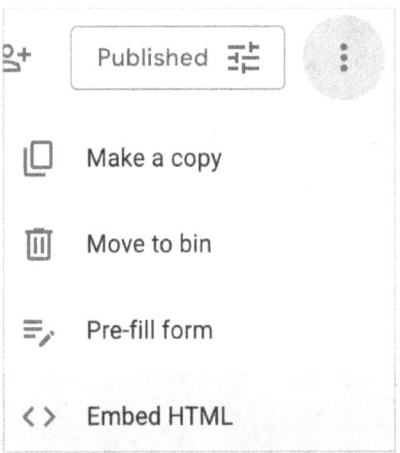

12: Quizzes

In this chapter, we're going to look at the quiz option in Forms. It's an easy way to create tests and exams, and to provide instant feedback, for example, to students.

Questions	Responses	Settings

Settings – The global settings are set here.

Questions - The bulk of the work is here, where you tell Forms which answers are correct and set the points per question. You can also set up automatic feedback for correct or incorrect answers, including links to websites, documents or YouTube videos.

Responses - This is where the analysis happens after your respondents have filled out the quiz. You can see summary information for all the responses. We'll look at this in detail in the next chapter.

Creating a quiz
To create a quiz, you first need to turn the quiz function on. Go to the Settings menu. Then turn on "Make this a quiz".

Make this a quiz
Assign point values, set answers and automatically provide feedback

This opens a set of options below, which are global settings for the quiz. There are 3 sections: Release marks, Respondent settings, Global quiz defaults.

Release marks - Here you have the choice of either allowing the respondent to see their mark as soon as they submit the form or you may decide to send it to them at a later date.

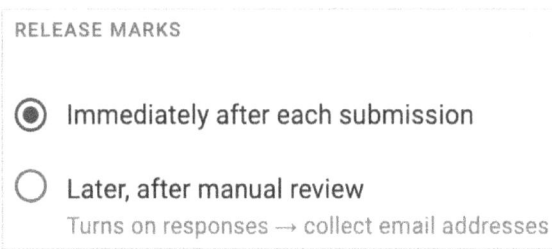

The latter is useful if you have questions which require your review first. For example, they are written answers, or you may decide to let everyone know their scores at the same time once everyone has filled in the form. To do this, the email collection is automatically turned on, so that the score can be emailed to them.

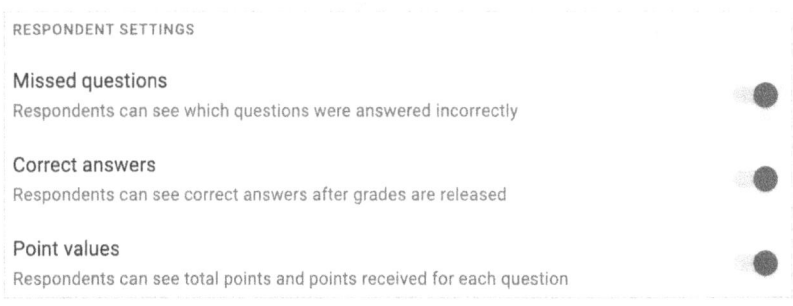

Respondent settings – This part is controlling what the respondent can see when they see their marks. You can show them the answers they got wrong ("missed questions"), the answer key ("Correct answers"), and how many points have been awarded per question.

Default question point value	1 points
Point values for every new question	

Global quiz defaults – Here, you can set the default points value for each question. By default, it's set as 1 point.

Setting up the questions in the quiz
Add the questions to the form, then it's time to tell Forms which questions are correct, etc. Click on the "Questions" tab.

Here, we can see that the email address collection has been added to the top of the form. You can't move this.

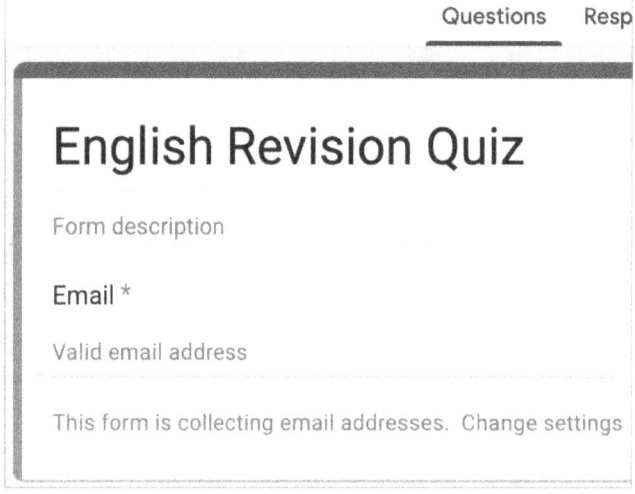

Add a question as normal. As you can see, at the bottom of the question, you have "Answer key". Click on that to enter edit the answer key.

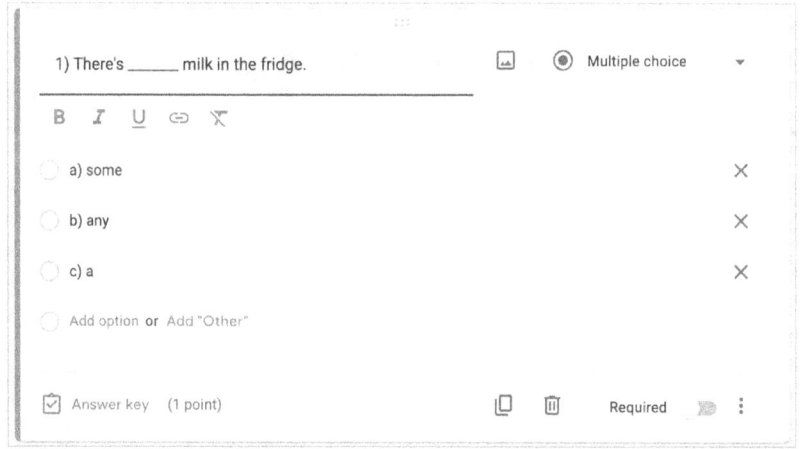

It'll prompt you to choose a correct answer or answers. Just click on the answer(s) that is correct.

You can also set the points value for the question.

The default value is set in Settings.

You'll then have your correct answer highlighted and the points value. If you select the wrong answer, click it again to remove it.

Adding feedback to your answers

You have the option to add automatic feedback to your questions. Click on "Add Answer Feedback". You can leave feedback for incorrect answers and/or correct answers.

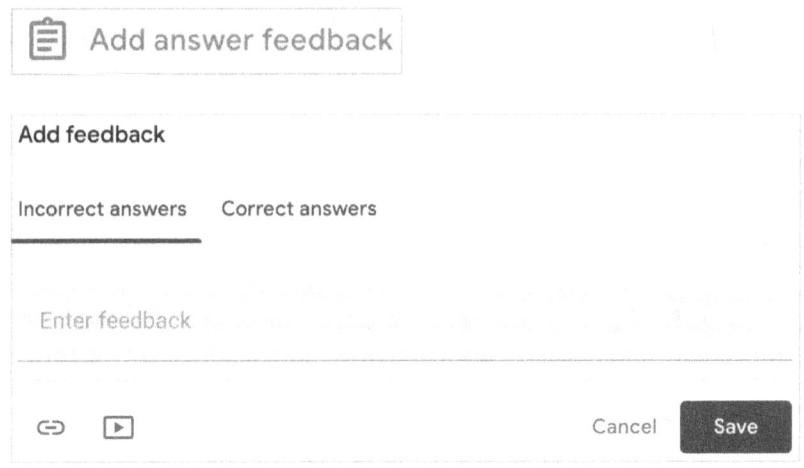

To add feedback just type in the box, where it says "Enter feedback".

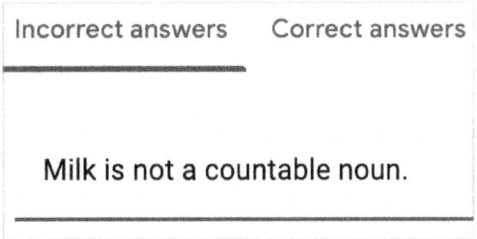

You do the same for the correct answers, just by clicking on the "Correct answers" tab.

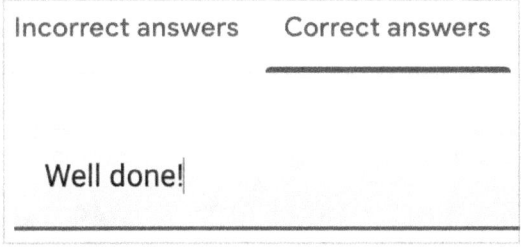

Not only can you leave text feedback but you can also add links. This is particularly nice, if you want to direct the student to some further reading related to the question or to some extra help.

Click on the link icon.

There are two parts: "Link to" is where you paste in your link, and "Text to display" is where you add the name of the link, i.e. what the respondent sees to click on.

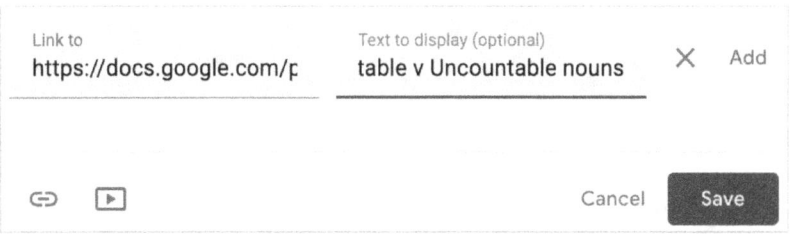

Here, I've pasted in a link to a Google Doc with an explanation of this particular grammar point. The link can be to anything, YouTube video, a website, images, etc. Click "Add" then "Save".

It shows you that this question has a link added to it.

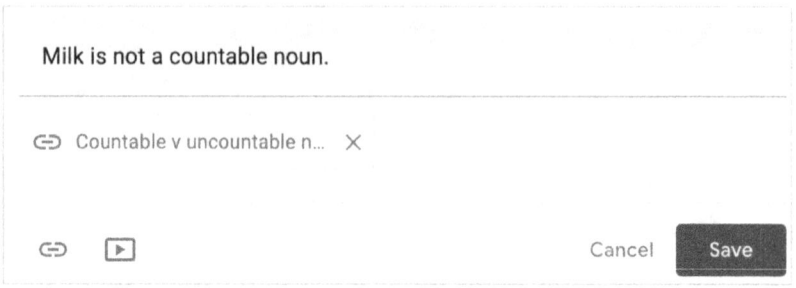

Milk is not a countable noun.

🔗 Countable v uncountable n... ✕

🔗 ▶ Cancel Save

Adding a YouTube video in the feedback to your answers

You can also search for a YouTube video and add a link to it. Click on the YouTube icon.

Type in the topic you're looking for, or if you have it, the URL. Double-click on the video you want.

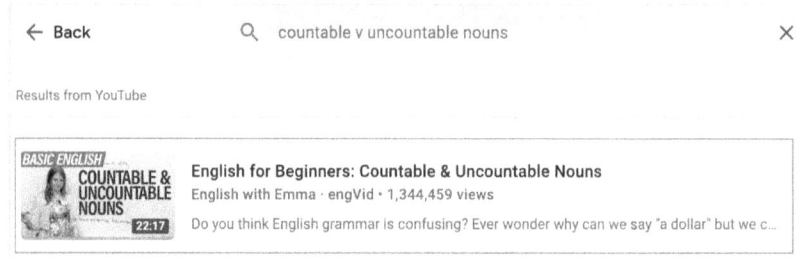

← Back 🔍 countable v uncountable nouns ✕

Results from YouTube

English for Beginners: Countable & Uncountable Nouns
English with Emma · engVid · 1,344,459 views
Do you think English grammar is confusing? Ever wonder why can we say "a dollar" but we c...

This will add it to the question feedback. Click "Save" to add it.

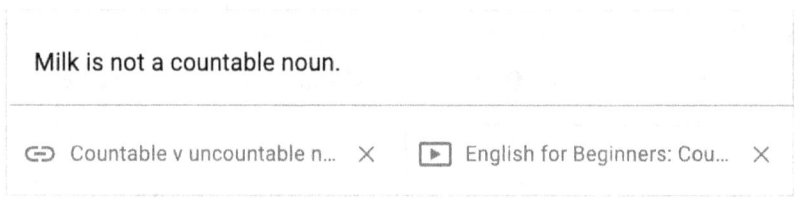

Milk is not a countable noun.

🔗 Countable v uncountable n... ✕   ▶ English for Beginners: Cou... ✕

So, now we have a question which will self-correct and provide feedback if the student gets it right or wrong, and gives them extra material to check out, if they need to understand it further.

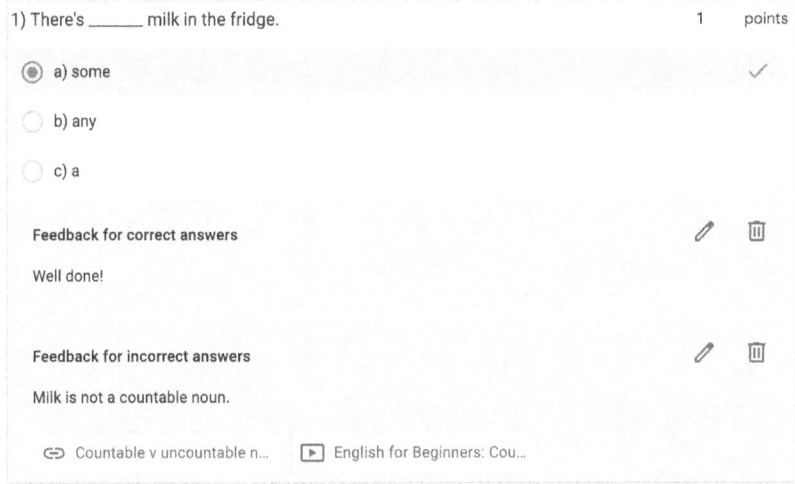

13: Quizzes – Responses & Scores

In this chapter we're going to continue looking at quizzes and in particular, what we can do once our quiz is completed.

Reviewing the summary of responses

Once you receive some responses, you will want to review and analyse them. Forms provides three main ways, either looking at the summary of all the responses, by question, or by the individual responses. Let's look at the "summary" first of all. Click on the "Responses" tab. Then if not already selected, click on the "Summary" tab.

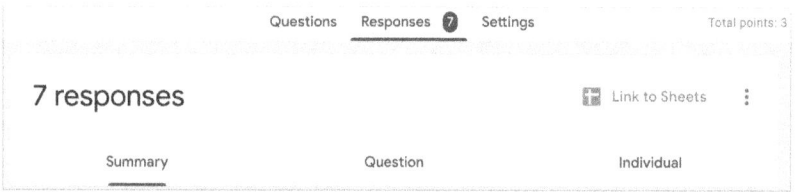

Under Insights, you'll see the average (mean), median and range of the responses. Then underneath, a graph showing you the spread of the results.

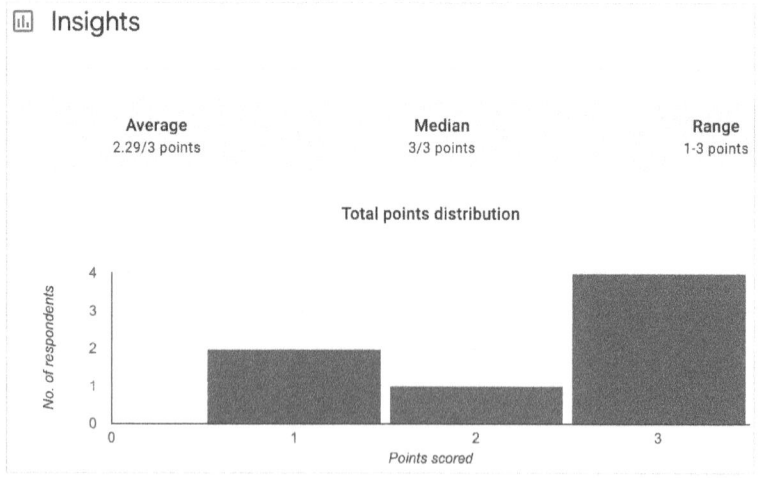

Then you have the list of respondents, their total scores and when their scores were released. This is ordered by the release date. This is a nice, quick summary which will help you identify who needs help.

☑ Scores		Release scores
Email	Score/4	Score released
baz@bazroberts.com	4	2 May 20:53
baz@bazroberts.com (1)	1	2 May 20:54
baz@bazroberts.com (2)	3	2 May 20:54
baz@bazroberts.com (3)	4	2 May 20:54

From this table, you can click on a line to go directly to that individual's responses to see where they need help.

Sending emails to respondents with their responses and the answer key
If the email setting was selected earlier, you can also send the students a copy of their responses along with the correct answers and feedback, by clicking on "Release Scores".

☑ Scores		Release scores
Email	Score/3	Score released
baz@bazroberts.com	3	19 Dec 20:17 ↻
baz@bazroberts.com (1)	1	19 Dec 20:17 ↻

This opens up the Release Scores dialogue box. In here you can add a message to the respondents and then click on who you want to send the emails to.

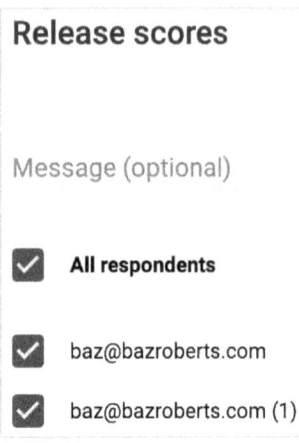

By default, all of the respondents are selected. Then click "Send Emails and Release".

You can do this whether you selected earlier so that they can see their result immediately or later.

Finally, you can also look at the summary of each question, to see not only which ones are causing problems but also what alternative answers the respondents are choosing. This is the part I find most useful.

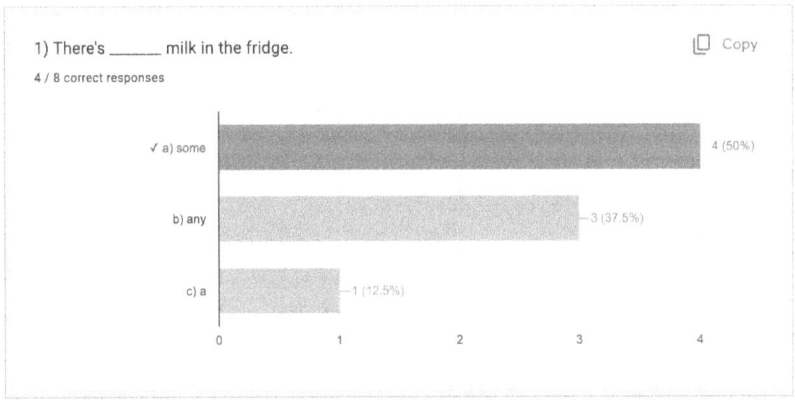

1) There's _____ milk in the fridge.

4 / 8 correct responses

- ✓ a) some — 4 (50%)
- b) any — 3 (37.5%)
- c) a — 1 (12.5%)

Reviewing responses by question

Next, you can summarise the responses by question. Click on the "Question" tab.

Question

You can click through the questions by clicking on the arrows next to for example, 1 of 3.

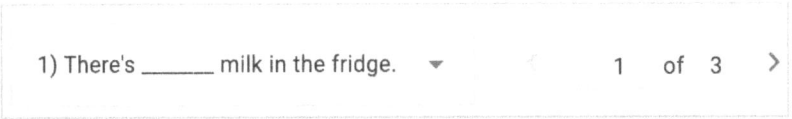

1) There's _____ milk in the fridge.   ▾   ‹   1   of   3   ›

You can also go straight to a question by selecting it from the drop-down menu.

For each question, you have the option of viewing the options and it also shows you the correct and incorrect answers.

91

1) There's _____ milk in the fridge.   Hide options ∧

⦿ a) some   ✓

○ b) any   ✕

○ c) a   ✕

Here you have the option of selecting whether a question is right or wrong, which can be useful for written in answers, where there may be various possibilities.

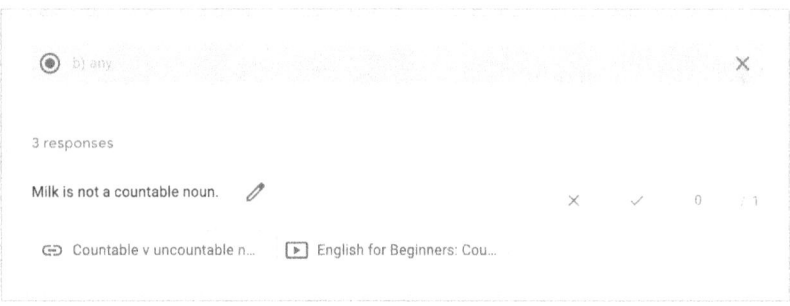

Reviewing individual responses

To see each individual's response, click on the "Individual" tab.

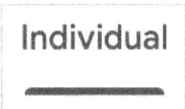

It shows you each response in chronological order. It shows their email address, the response number, gives you the possibility of printing it, and deleting it. To navigate through them, either click on the arrows or double-click on the number in the box and type in the response number you want.

baz@bazroberts.com   ▾   1   of 8   ›   🖨 🗑

Below that it shows you the score for that respondent, if the score has already been released to them or not, and the option to release the score.

Release score

By default, clicking on Release score will just select that one student to email, although you can send scores to others by ticking their checkboxes.

Underneath it shows the questions, with whether they got them right or wrong, plus it shows the correct answers, any feedback that you set up, and any links that you added earlier. This is exactly how the respondents see it, when the score is released.

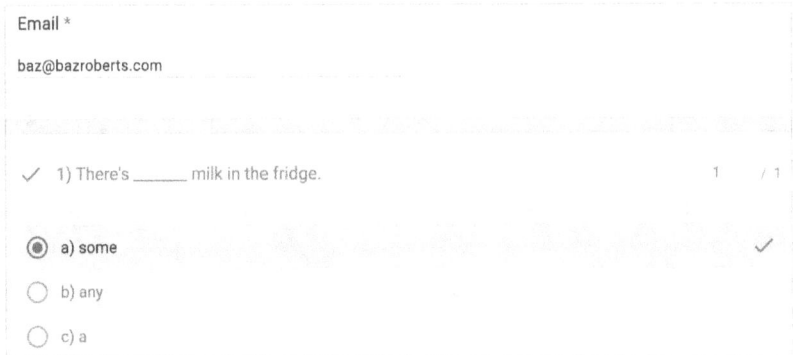

Email *

baz@bazroberts.com

✓   1) There's _____ milk in the fridge.   1   / 1

◉ a) some   ✓

○ b) any

○ c) a

You also have the option of adding individual feedback, by clicking on "Add individual feedback" under any of the questions.

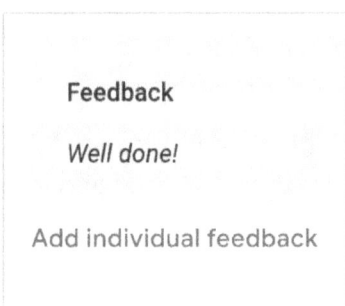

This can be useful if you haven't set up any automatic feedback or if you have questions that can't be automatically corrected, for example, a piece of written text.

Type in your feedback and if you want, you can add a link like we saw earlier. Then press "Save".

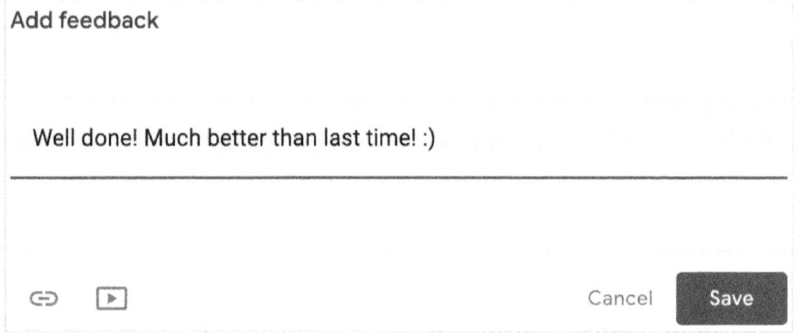

Then you'll be prompted to save all the edits you've made.

How can respondents see their score?

If the "release mark immediately" option was selected earlier, when the respondent submits the forms, on the confirmation page, they will have the option "View your score".

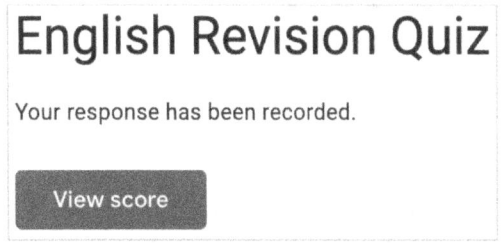

Clicking on that will take them to the form filled in with their answers, and depending on the options you chose, will have the answer key and feedback.

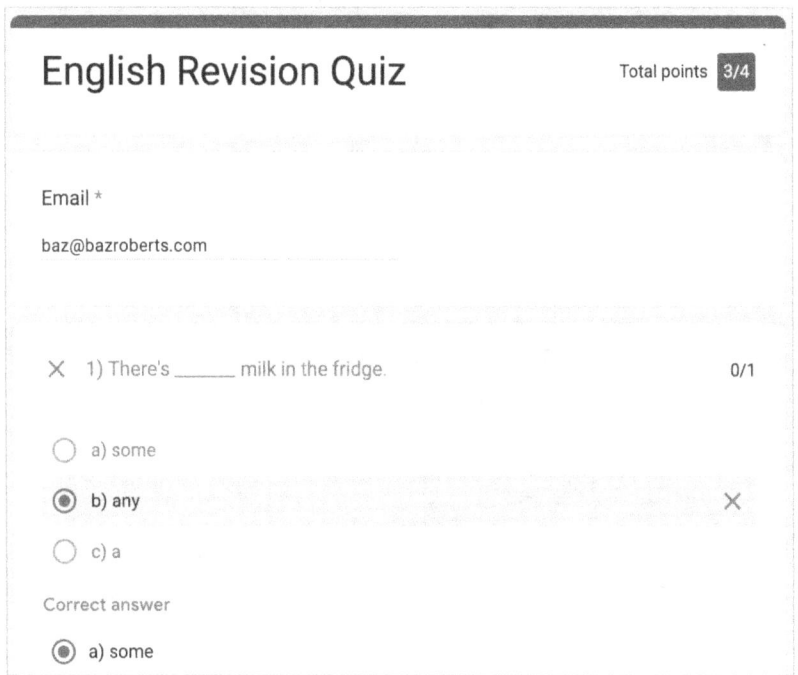

Feedback

Milk is not a countable noun.

You can see that the YouTube video and document link we set up earlier are shown to the respondents.

The other way I mentioned above is that they receive an email when the scores are released. This is the email they receive:

Your score has been released for English Revision Quiz.

English Revision Quiz

1 / 4

VIEW

It contains their total and then when they click on "View", it takes them to the form filled out with their answers and depending on the options you chose when setting up the quiz, the answer key, feedback and any links you added.

This means that they have a permanent copy to review, which is better than only seeing it when they submit the form.

14: Uploading files via Forms

Forms allows you to upload files directly to your Google Drive, which can be an easy way to receive files directly into your Drive.

It allows users to upload documents via a Google Form and then those documents are uploaded to the form owner's Drive. Note, the user needs to be logged into a Google account to use the facility.

In the example below, a teacher wants his/her students to upload a picture of their family, ready for the next lesson where they will talk about them. The beauty of this is that the students only need the URL of the form.

Setting up the form
Create a form and add a question then from the drop-down menu choose the "File upload" option.

This will display some information and a warning. Choosing this option allows the form-filler to upload files directly to your Drive, so use it with care. Click continue.

Let respondents upload files to Drive

Files will be uploaded to the form owner's Google Drive. Respondents will be required to sign in to Google when file upload questions are added to a form. Please only share this form with people you trust.

Cancel   Continue

This will add the file upload 'question' to your form. You will be presented with various options.

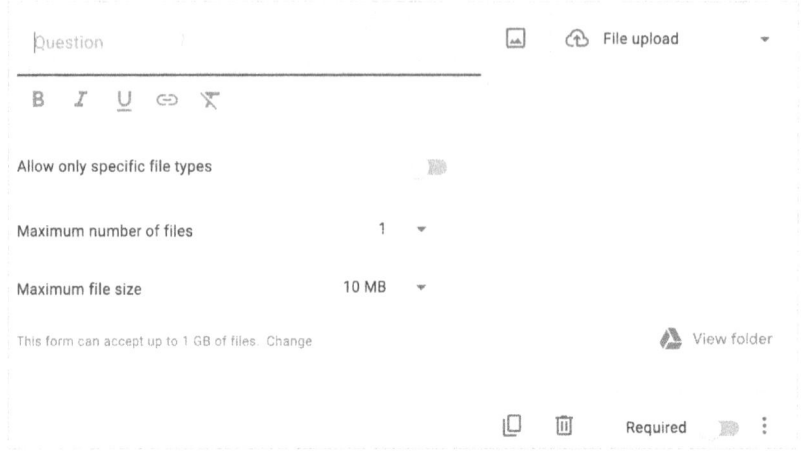

First, change the 'Question' title. This can be an instruction, a title or a question.

Next, we have the option to limit the file type. As in this example, I only want photos to be sent, so I click the toggle next to "Allow only specific file types".

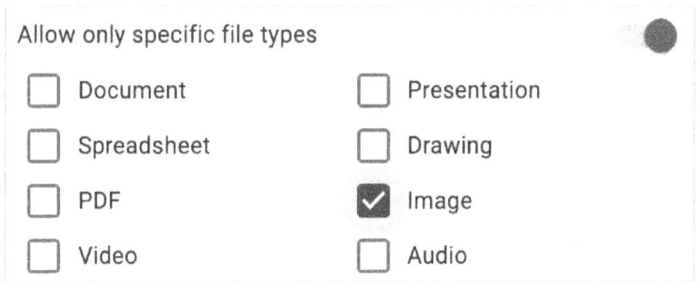

Then I tick the file type I want. Note, Image will allow different types of image files, e.g. jpgs, pngs, tifs, etc.

Next, we have the option of limiting the number of files that can be uploaded by the user. By default, it's only 1 but it can be changed to a maximum of 5 or 10.

Maximum number of files		1
Maximum file size	10	5
This form can accept up to 1 GB of files. Change		10

We also have the option of controlling the file size that can be uploaded. The default is 10MB but this can be reduced to 1MB or increased up to 10GB.

Maximum number of files	1 MB
Maximum file size	10 MB
This form can accept up to 1 GB of files. Change	100 MB
	1 GB
	10 GB

Finally, we can limit the space the files will take up on our Drive. By default, this is 1GB. To change it, click Change.

This opens the Settings menu. At the bottom, click on the drop-down menu and select the size you want.

FILE UPLOAD

Total size limit for all uploaded files Responses will not be accepted after the limit is reached. Learn more	1 GB
	10 GB
	100 GB
:sentation nage how the form and responses are presented	1 TB

If the limit is reached, you'll receive a notification email telling you it's been reached and that no more files will be accepted.

Uploading a file from your computer
Click on the form URL to open the form in the responder view. The form will display a message checking with the user, which account they want to upload the files from. To change the account, they click "Switch accounts", then will need to sign out and sign back in with the different account.

To upload a file, click "Add File".

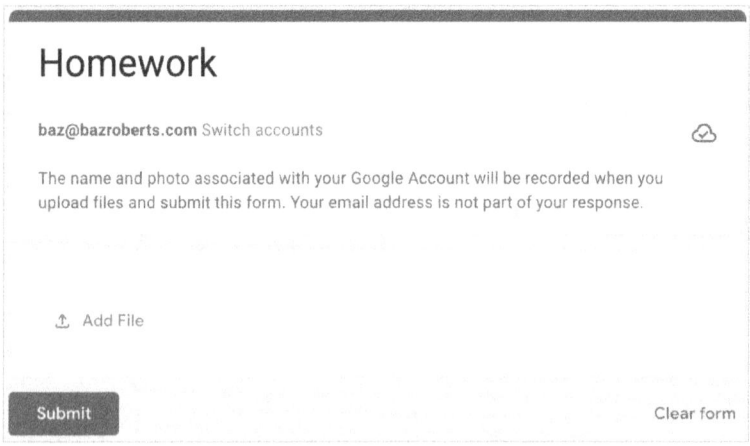

This opens the Insert file dialogue box. There are 3 options, upload a file from your computer (or device), upload it from your My Drive, or choose one which has been recently uploaded. Let's upload a photo from my computer.

In the Upload tab, click "Browse". Alternatively, you can drag a file onto the page to upload it.

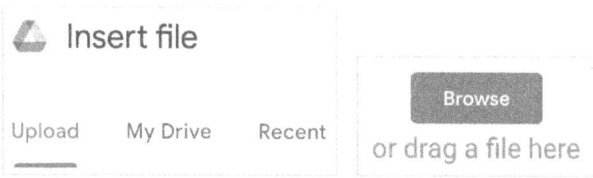

Select the file you want and click "Open".

This will then show you the file name uploaded. If the form allows it, you can add more files, by clicking on "Add file" again.

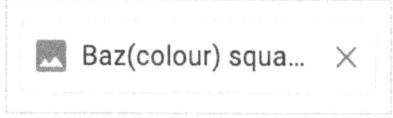

Once ready, click on "Submit". You will receive the usual form submission confirmation message.

Uploading from My Drive
You can also upload a file from your My Drive. After clicking "Add File", click on the My Drive tab, find your file, click on it and click "Insert". As before, click "Submit" to upload it.

Where do the files go?

The files will be uploaded to the form owner's Drive and your own My Drive. You can access the folder either via the form Questions or Responses tab or directly on your Drive.

Opening the Responses tab, you can see what files have been uploaded. You can open the files directly from this page by clicking on the file name.

To go to the folder click "View folder". Note, you can delete the files from this page by deleting the individual response.

When the file upload question is added it creates two folders. One for the form and a sub-folder within it for the question.

So, in our example, it's created this folder for the form.

13-Homework - File upload (File responses)

Then within it, it's created this folder which is linked to the question. In there are the uploaded images.

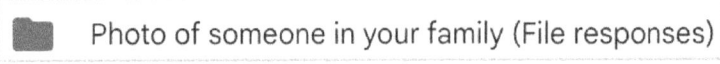

in the same folder where the form is, with the form's name plus "(File responses)".

The files will have the file name they were uploaded with and then the name of the account that was used to upload it.

This is a great, easy way to send someone files, without the need to share Drive folders, use Classroom, etc. The automatic creation of folders is a helpful feature, which keeps things organised without any effort on your part.

Note, that the files that are uploaded are added to your Drive (as well as the form sender's) and files which are not Google documents (PDFs, photos, etc) will take up the form owner's Drive space.

15: Importing questions

In this chapter, we're going to see how we can import questions and sections from a previously-made form. This is a great time-saver. Open the form you want to import into, and then from the Questions section, click on the import question icon.

Click on the form you want to import the questions from and click "Select".

This will open the Import questions sidebar. Here you can select all the parts or select certain ones to import into your form.

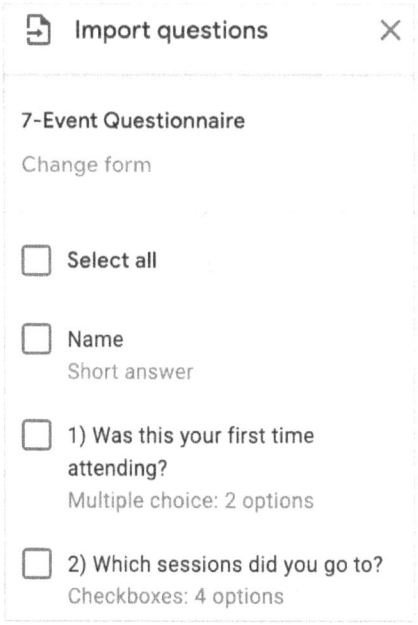

If you select a section, it selects all the questions and images in that section. You can always untick anything you don't want to import.

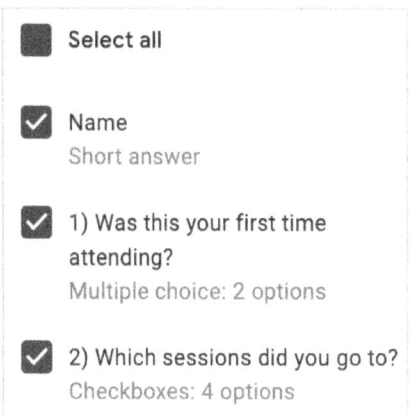

Then click Import questions.

Import questions (3)

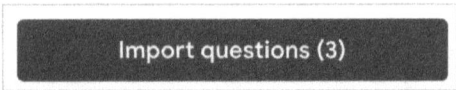

This will import all the parts you've selected into your form.

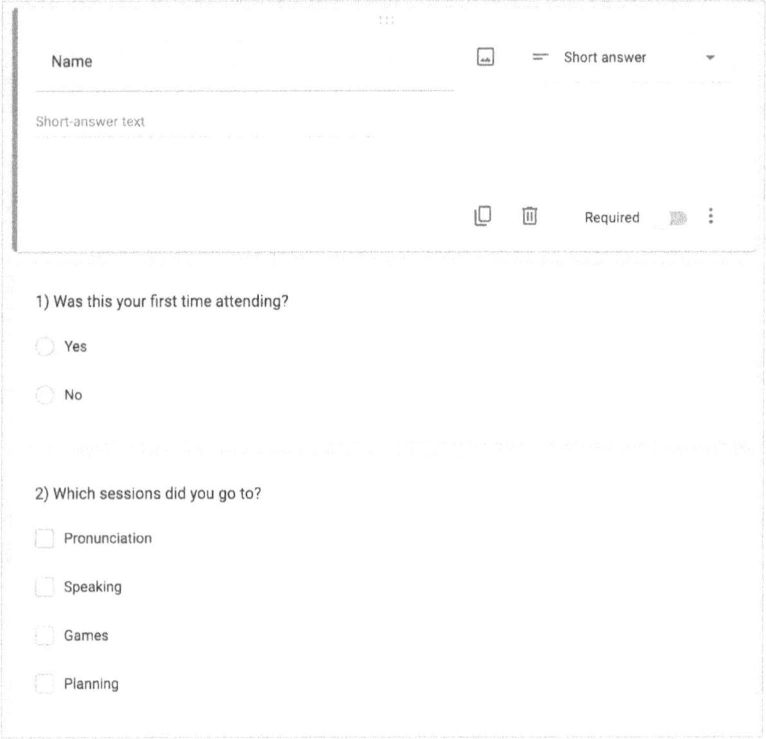
Name
Short answer
Short-answer text
Required
1) Was this your first time attending?
Yes
No
2) Which sessions did you go to?
Pronunciation
Speaking
Games
Planning

16: Pre-filled Google Forms

Sometimes we want to pre-fill parts of a form out. Why would we want to do that?

- It's quicker for the person to fill out your form
- To ensure the information is in the format you want
- The data format is consistent so that it's easier to analyse afterwards
- It contains information that the form-filler doesn't know
- It adds the personal touch, if you add their name on it
- One form can collect data from many sources, and be sorted with ease later on in the same spreadsheet

As an example, I've created a simple end-of-course questionnaire for our students. I want to include the group name, level, teacher, and classroom, so that I can use the same form for all the different groups. To make sure the data I receive is consistent, and so that it's quicker for the students to fill out, I want to pre-fill those parts.

The first step once you've made the form is to go to the 3-dot menu and select "Get pre-filled link".

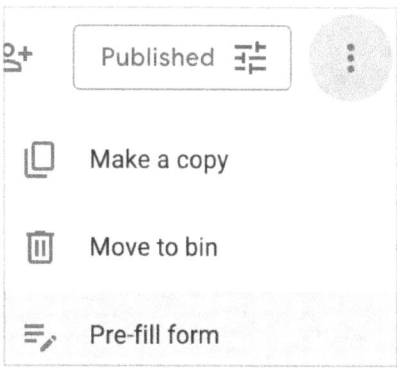

This opens the form ready for you to pre-fill. Fill in the fields you want to pre-fill. Then click "Get link".

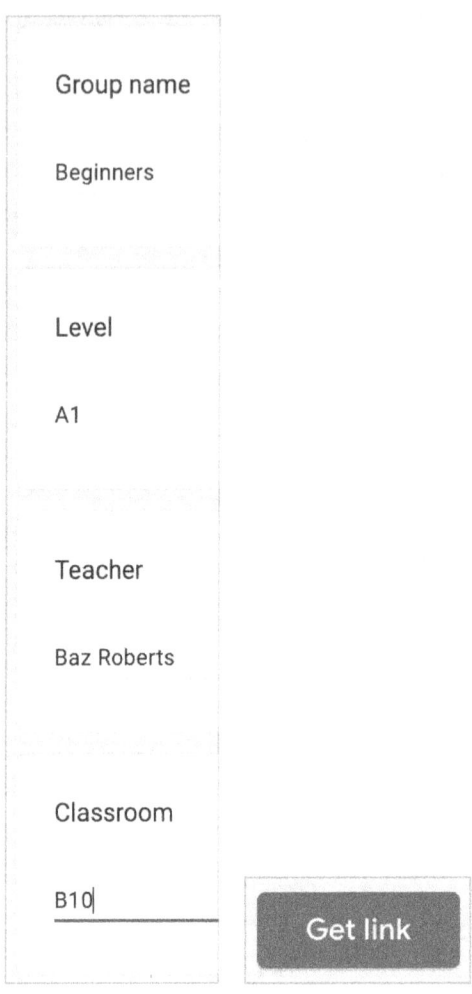

Group name

Beginners

Level

A1

Teacher

Baz Roberts

Classroom

B10|

Get link

A black bar will appear, then click COPY LINK to the clipboard.

| Share this link to include pre-filled responses | COPY LINK |

If you paste that link into the browser, you will see it has pre-filled the first four questions.

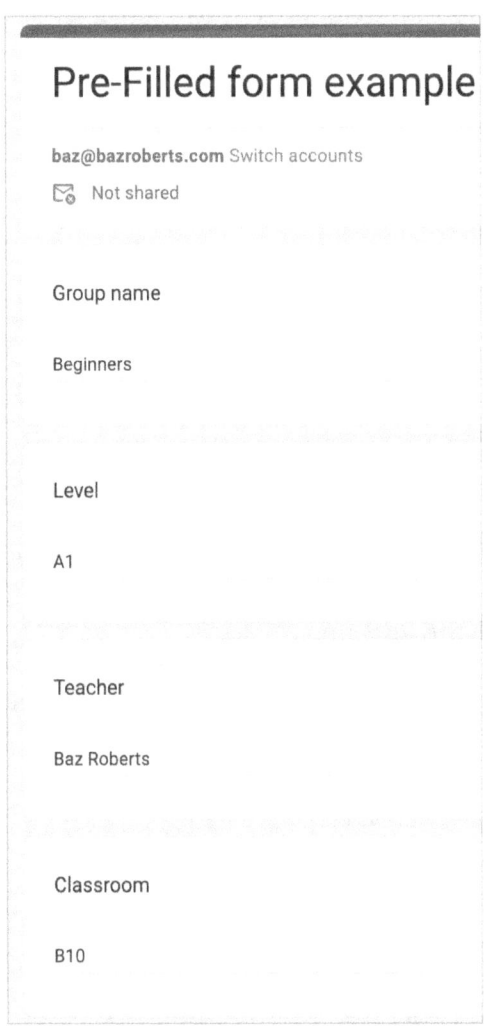

Pre-Filled form example

baz@bazroberts.com Switch accounts

Not shared

Group name

Beginners

Level

A1

Teacher

Baz Roberts

Classroom

B10

The student would then just fill in the feedback questions. When we receive the responses from the students, we can easily analyse them by group name, level, teacher, and classroom.

17: Installing an add-on

As hopefully you've seen so far in this book, Google Forms is a wonderfully easy way to create forms but it does have some limitations. Fortunately, some of those gaps are filled by add-ons, which are programs which extend the functionality of Forms.

Installing an add-on
Click on the 3-dot menu in the edit view and "Get add-ons" to open the Google Workspace marketplace which shows add-ons that work with Google Forms.

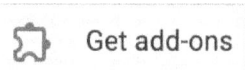 Get add-ons

Here you find a wide range of add-ons. Let's install a Chat GPT-related one, which allows you to create form questions based on a text. Click on the add-on.

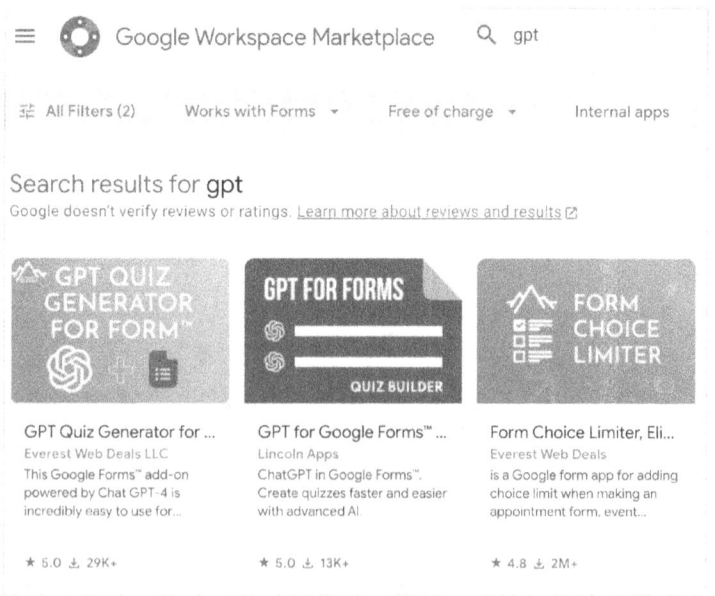

≡ ◯ Google Workspace Marketplace   🔍 gpt

⇶ All Filters (2)   Works with Forms ▾   Free of charge ▾   Internal apps

Search results for gpt

Google doesn't verify reviews or ratings. Learn more about reviews and results ↗

GPT QUIZ GENERATOR FOR FORM™

GPT FOR FORMS — QUIZ BUILDER

FORM CHOICE LIMITER

GPT Quiz Generator for ...
Everest Web Deals LLC
This Google Forms™ add-on powered by Chat GPT-4 is incredibly easy to use for...

★ 5.0 ⬇ 29K+

GPT for Google Forms™ ...
Lincoln Apps
ChatGPT in Google Forms™. Create quizzes faster and easier with advanced AI

★ 5.0 ⬇ 13K+

Form Choice Limiter, Eli...
Everest Web Deals
is a Google form app for adding choice limit when making an appointment form, event...

★ 4.8 ⬇ 2M+

It will take you to the add-on information page. At the top you have the options to install it.

GPT Quiz Generator ...

This Google Forms™ add-on powered by Chat GPT-4 is incredibly easy to use for generating quiz tests. You need to do is enter your text article and click the "Generate...

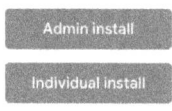

Normally, it will be an individual install, which only installs it to your account but if you have a business or education account, you may be able to install it for all the domain, meaning everyone in the domain will be able to use it.

Below shows you how many people have installed it and the current rating and number of reviews.

Next, in Overview you can see screen shots, videos, and information about the add-on.

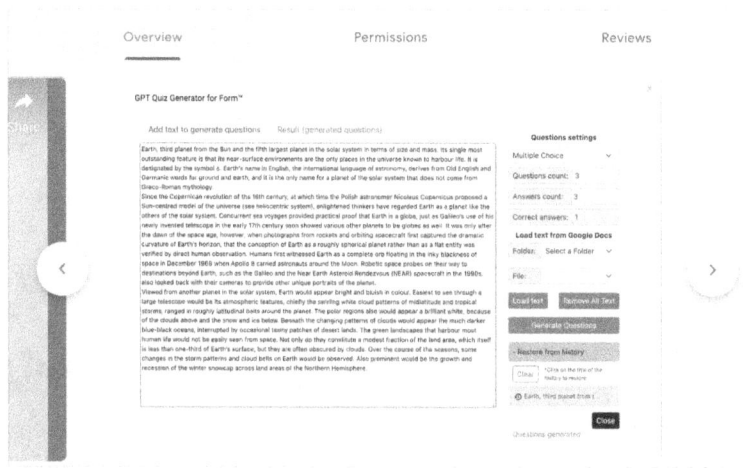

OK, so let's install the add-on. Click "Individual install".

Click Continue.

 Get ready to install

GPT Quiz Generator for Form... needs your
permission in order to start installing.

By clicking Continue, you acknowledge that your
information will be used in accordance with the terms of
service and privacy policy of this application.

CANCEL   CONTINUE

Select the account you want to add it to.

**Choose an account from
bazroberts.com**

to continue to GPT Quiz Generator for Forms™

 **Barrie Roberts**
baz@bazroberts.com

It will give you a summary of what the add-on will do and the
permissions it needs. Authorise it by clicking "Allow".

You will then see a confirmation message, telling you it's
installed. Click Done.

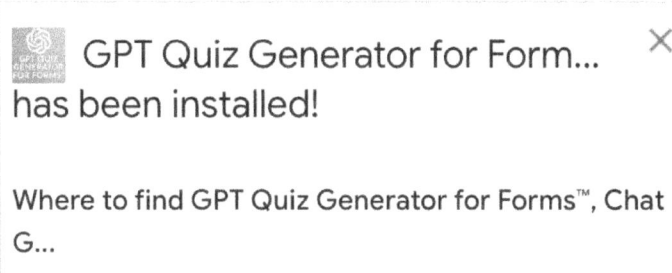

GPT Quiz Generator for Form... ✕
has been installed!

Where to find GPT Quiz Generator for Forms™, Chat
G...

Using an add-on
Click on the add-ons menu (puzzle icon) at the top of the
page and select the add-on you want.

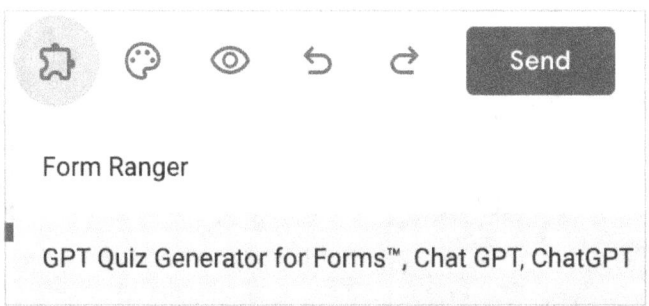

Form Ranger

GPT Quiz Generator for Forms™, Chat GPT, ChatGPT

This particular add-on needs you to get an API key from the
Open AI site. Most add-ons also come with a Help menu.

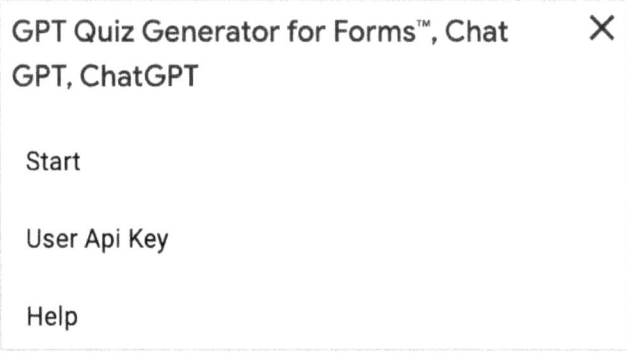

GPT Quiz Generator for Forms™, Chat ✕
GPT, ChatGPT

Start

User Api Key

Help

Uninstalling an add-on

To uninstall an add-on, open the Google Workspace marketplace by clicking on the 3-dot menu and selecting "Get add-ons".

Then click on the gear icon and select Manage Apps.

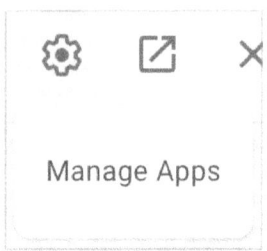

Click on the 3-dot menu on the app you want to uninstall.

Then click Uninstall. Then click Uninstall app.

Final note from the author

If you have any questions about the content of this book, then please contact me at baz@bazroberts.com

FEEDBACK
I would love to hear your thoughts on this book! It would be great, if you could spare a minute to fill in this short feedback form: bit.ly/BazsBooks

Finally, a big thank you for buying this book. I really do hope it has helped you use Google Forms. Thank you!

Barrie "Baz" Roberts

Rev 22

Books and ebooks available by this author:

GOOGLE WORKSPACE

- Beginner's Guide to Google Sheets
- Google Sheet Functions – A step-by-step guide
- Google Sheets Function 2
- Beginner's Guide to Google Docs
- Beginner's Guide to Google Drive
- Step-by-step Guide to Google Forms
- Step-by-step Guide to Google Sites
- Step-by-step Guide to Google Slides
- Step-by-step Guide to Google Meet

APPS SCRIPT

Expand the functionality of the Google Workspace apps, like Google Forms, by learning **Google Apps Script**, which can automate them. Yes, it's possible to automate the creation of Google Forms and to automate the managing of form responses!

- Beginner's Guide to Google Apps Script 1 - Sheets
- Beginner's Guide to Google Apps Script 2 - Forms
- Beginner's Guide to Google Apps Script 3 - Drive
- Step-by-step Guide to Google Apps Script 4 - Documents
- Google Apps Script Projects 1
- Google Apps Script Projects 2
- JavaScript Fundamentals for Apps Script Users

I also post and share articles, news and information related to Google Workspace and Apps Script on my website www.bazroberts.com and I post on social media:

X: barrielroberts
Bluesky: bazroberts.bsky.social
Medium: @bazroberts
LinkedIn: bazroberts
Instagram: bazroberts_googleworkspace

www.ingramcontent.com/pod-product-compliance
Lightning Source LLC
Chambersburg PA
CBHW070355220526
45467CB00001B/395